Los Árabes
of New Mexico
Compadres from a Distant Land

Los Árabes of New Mexico
Compadres from a Distant Land

Monika Ghattas

SUNSTONE PRESS

SANTA FE

© 2012 by Monika Ghattas
All Rights Reserved.

No part of this book may be reproduced in any form or by any electronic or mechanical means including information storage and retrieval systems without permission in writing from the publisher, except by a reviewer who may quote brief passages in a review.

Sunstone books may be purchased for educational, business, or sales promotional use. For information please write: Special Markets Department, Sunstone Press, P.O. Box 2321, Santa Fe, New Mexico 87504-2321.

Book and Cover design › Vicki Ahl
Body typeface › Palatino Linotype with Harrington
Printed on acid-free paper

Library of Congress Cataloging-in-Publication Data

Ghattas, Monika White.
  Los Árabes of New Mexico : compadres from a distant land / by Monika Ghattas.
     pages cm
  Includes bibliographical references and index.
  ISBN 978-0-86534-911-7 (softcover : alkaline paper)
 1. Syrian Americans--New Mexico--History. 2. Lebanese Americans--New Mexico--History. 3. Immigrants--New Mexico--History. 4. Syrian Americans--New Mexico--Social conditions. 5. Lebanese Americans--New Mexico--Social conditions. 6. New Mexico--Ethnic relations--History. 7. New Mexico--Emigration and immigration--History. 8. Syria--Emigration and immigration--History. 9. Lebanon--Emigration and immigration--History. I. Title.
  F805.S98G42 2012
  305.8009789--dc23
                                        2012038320

WWW.SUNSTONEPRESS.COM
SUNSTONE PRESS / POST OFFICE BOX 2321 / SANTA FE, NM 87504-2321 /USA
(505) 988-4418 / ORDERS ONLY (800) 243-5644 / FAX (505) 988-1025

Dedication

To those Intrepid Travelers
who Settled in this Enchanted Land

Contents

Acknowledgments _____ 9
Introduction _____ 11

1 Syria and Mount Lebanon in the Late Nineteenth Century ___ 19
2 Immigrating to the New World _____ 25
3 Walking Bazaars: The Peddlers _____ 43
4 From Sojourners to Settlers _____ 55
5 In Search of Economic Opportunities _____ 89
6 Assimilation: Soy Mexicano casi _____ 115
7 From Shopkeepers to Entrepreneurs _____ 128
8 The Women: Resilience and Resourcefulness _____ 147
Conclusion _____ 155

Notes _____ 159
Bibliography _____ 175
Name Index _____ 185

Acknowledgments

This book is a composite of many voices; some of the storytellers are no longer with us, but many others will read this narrative and recognize their personal contributions. My thanks to all of you, especially to those who made a special effort to help me locate resources and answer my questions. The late Brahaim Hindi, Jr., spent an entire day with me in Duran, New Mexico, recounting his family's experiences in this small New Mexico community. The multiple relationships between the early Roumieh families would have been difficult to understand without the help of Jay Sahd, while Viola Sanchez strove tirelessly to locate materials on the Tabet families. I appreciate the ongoing support and interest in this project of Nick Abdalla and Toby Michael.

I am grateful for the library resources that were available and the help I received in locating documents and incidental information. A special thank you goes to David Schneider at the Albuquerque Public Library, who not only advised and assisted me with procuring information, but also was unfailing in his enthusiasm and promotion of this project. In Beirut I was fortunate to have the help of Elias Choueiry in the Jafet library of the American University; in addition, I would like to acknowledge the encouragement of the Lebanese Emigration Research Center (LERC) at Notre Dame University in Kesrwan, Lebanon.

The National Endowment for the Humanities workshop on immigration, 'Landmarks in American History,' that I attended at Case Western Reserve University under the direction of John Grabowski made me aware of the complex history and varied interpretations of the immigrant experience. The discussions about the relationship between history and heritage were especially useful for this study based in large part on oral history.

My thanks to Marc Simmons and Henry Tobias for taking the time to read this material and sending me their encouraging commentary. I am especially grateful to Philip Kayal and Gary Nabhan who reviewed this manuscript carefully and made valuable observations on content and themes. And I appreciate the information Gary Nabhan shared with me about the culture and history of the Syrian community in the Southwest.

The meticulous editing and good advice of Dawn Hall made this manuscript a more manageable and coherent document.

I would like to acknowledge the docent program at the Albuquerque Museum of Art and History that has expanded my understanding and my appreciation of the rich and multifaceted history of New Mexico.

I thank my family for their patience and especially my husband who listened endlessly to my tales, translated documents whenever necessary and frequently accompanied me on my travels to uncover this story—I appreciate your interest and your engagement in this project.

Introduction

The Budagher exit on the highway between Santa Fe and Albuquerque is located about midway between the two cities. It is named after Joseph Budagher, who homesteaded here in the early 1930s after the road connecting the two cities was moved several miles to the east, bypassing his business in Domingo. Today nothing remains of the curio shop, the saloon, or the gas pumps. Even the former marketplace center that was erected in the 1990s has lost its tenants. Budagher, whose original name was Abu Dagher, belonged to a small group of Arabic speaking immigrants who settled in New Mexico between the late 1880s and the early 1920s. Many of them have been woven into the multicultural tapestry of New Mexico history so seamlessly that their ethnic identity has almost disappeared. This study calls attention to their presence and highlights their contributions to the storied voices of the Southwest.

About 20 percent of population growth in the US West in the early twentieth century is attributed to immigrants; however, not until fairly recently have American historians acknowledged immigrants' presence and their contributions to the development of the region.[1] In recent years several excellent books centered on specific immigrant groups in New Mexico have addressed this oversight. Especially noteworthy are Henry Tobias's *A History of the Jews in New Mexico* and Tomas Jaehn's *Germans in the Southwest, 1850–1920*. The history of the state's Italian community has also been documented in several books and oral history projects. These studies have focused on immigrant efforts to find a balance between assimilation and the preservation of an ethnic identity. In addition, scholars have noted and evaluated their role in the economic, political, and cultural growth of this area. This book about *Los Árabes* addresses some of the same issues.

The presence and eventual settlement of "los Árabes" has not been previously examined in depth for several reasons. Foremost, perhaps, is the fact that it is difficult to reconstruct the history of a small group of people who lacked a cohesive political or national identity. They most commonly characterized themselves by their religion, village origin, and family affiliation. Alixa Naff, the distinguished historian of the Arab experience in America, commented on "the flawed and inadequate understanding of the Syrian Americans of the social and political history of their forebears."[2] They seemingly knew little of their regional history, art or literature. Thus the preservation of an ethnic identity was not a priority; assimilation and economic success were decidedly more important.

Confusion over identity continues to this day among some second- and third-generation descendants. There is a concern that an Arab background implies contemporary political ideologies and/or national divisions instead of a shared linguistic and cultural heritage.[3] In fact, some Arab immigrants insist that they are Phoenicians, an idea popularized by the Arabic press in the early 1900s after a few Syrians living in the South were denied voting rights because they were considered nonwhite. When this controversy went to court, defendants tried to prove a connection to the ancient seafaring Phoenicians who were supposedly Caucasians. Then in later years many Phoenician clubs organized in the East and Midwest were dissolved over identity issues brought about by the division of Greater Syria into two distinct countries: Syria and Lebanon.

In New Mexico these immigrants dispersed over a wide area rather than maintaining an ethnic, cultural and geographic cohesion. The majority settled in Hispanic villages and in the burgeoning railroad and mining towns that sprung up in the late nineteenth and early twentieth centuries. Their relatively small number and distribution over a wide area precluded the establishment of specific educational, religious, and cultural institutions—like churches, schools, and social centers—that would have identified them as a separate community. Without the records these institutions customarily collect, it is difficult to reconstruct the lives and the experiences of these people. Area scholars did not record the presence of Syrian settlers or include them in local histories of early New Mexico communities.

Officials used a variety of ethnic labels to identify the Middle Eastern immigrants who arrived in New Mexico, as well as in most parts of the New World. In census records, for example, they were listed as Ottomans, Turks, Arabs, or Syrians. In a few instances they were even described as Persians, Greeks, and Armenians. Finally, in 1899 American immigration officials adopted a comprehensive and unified code that stated that they came from Turkey in Asia.

In the Hispanic villages of New Mexico they were known as "los Árabes." This form of reference will be used whenever their lives and acculturation are discussed in that context. In other instances, they will be referred to as Syrians, the form of identity they customarily used, because they came from the province of Syria in the Ottoman Empire. But in terms of current national boundaries, most of these immigrants came from Lebanon. Since that country did not become an independent nation until World War II, many did not call themselves Lebanese until more recent times. For the purposes of this work, Hispanics are the Spanish-speaking people of New Mexico.

The first Syrians came to New Mexico in the late 1880s; their numbers increased steadily until 1914, when the outbreak of World War I stopped all transatlantic travel. It was resumed in 1919, but the stringent new immigration laws of the Johnson-Reed Quota Act brought this flow to an end in 1924. Since the 1950s many more people from the Middle East have immigrated to this area; however, they are much more diverse in background, country of origin, and religion than the original group. This study is confined to an examination of Syrian immigration to New Mexico from the late 1880s to the beginning of World War II.

The phenomenon of chain migration is well illustrated in New Mexico; the majority of Syrian immigrants came from two specific locations: Roumieh, a village in Mount Lebanon, and Zahle, a small town located on the principal road between Beirut and Damascus. Thus most of the newcomers were small-scale farmers with some commercial experience that they had acquired through trade or limited merchandising. Contrary to some popular misconceptions, they had no connection to camels, tents, or a nomadic lifestyle.

Immigrant experiences are forged by many divergent forces; one of these is the coming together of two cultures. More than 90 percent of the Syrians who arrived in United States stayed in the East and Midwest where they encountered an industrialized society, an urban setting, and a predominately Anglo presence. In New Mexico, on the other hand, they came upon a generally preindustrial and rural environment infused with Hispanic culture and traditions. Thus the story of Syrian immigration in this part of the country is not a microcosm of what happened in other places; instead, it describes a distinctive process molded by existent conditions—a Middle Eastern people settling in Hispanic surroundings. This is foremost a story of cultural adaptation and not ethnic preservation.

Studies that focus on the economic success of immigrant groups emphasize the acute importance of timing. Immigrants' arrival must occur at a point when they can exploit opportunities that have recently opened. In Brazil, for example, many Syrians became quickly affluent because they entered a wholesale textile market that was on the verge of a massive expansion. In the United States Jewish immigrants already dominated this avenue. Here, the Industrial Revolution that needed unskilled labor for its prodigious expansion absorbed the Middle Eastern immigrants coming to the United States.

Yet New Mexico did not follow the national example; the Industrial Revolution bypassed the area. Yet it offered unique economic opportunities that were available to these people who arrived with little education and few if any material resources. To begin with Middle Eastern immigrants worked as peddlers, traversing the state with their goods and servicing outlying localities, remote ranches, and Indian pueblos. Then as the railroad expanded throughout the region and stimulated significant economic growth, they established small retail businesses in railroad and mining communities, as well as in Hispanic villages. Familiar with raising sheep, several Syrian families participated in New Mexico's traditional wool industry.

In the 1920s and 1930s a number of Syrians became entrepreneurs, investing in new technologies, such as movies, automobiles, and other forms of entertainment. At the same time, they foresaw the economic potential of tourism and promoted the construction of hotels and adjunct services.

Aside from favorable economic circumstances, they encountered other conditions that eased assimilation. Lacking in the state was a rigid social structure, one that could have inhibited social mobility. Immigrant contacts were primarily with the Hispanic community, which accepted them readily and allowed them to adapt to a familiar lifestyle with relative ease. Interestingly, the newcomers' Hispanic neighbors did not see them as Anglos.

Likewise, New Mexico's political culture at the turn of the nineteenth century was in a state of transition and not rigidly defined; thus participation in public life was open to the newcomers. It is noteworthy that several first-generation Syrian immigrants held political and community positions in New Mexico years before their countrymen could do so in other parts of the country.

The nature and quality of resources available for this study have resulted in a story that is more descriptive than analytical. A large and varied number of interviews will sketch the fundamental outline of these immigrant lives in New Mexico. Included are a few interviews with original settlers, but most of the informants were second- and third-generation descendants. Clearly this type of material must be approached with some care. Recollections are often laced with subtle biases and unwarranted concerns about privacy and propriety, while the reconstruction of the past to fit more modern parameters is an ongoing process. The dividing line between exaggeration and enthusiasm was occasionally difficult to discern. Sometimes the most valuable information came from incidental remarks or comments made in an offhand fashion. Nevertheless, these oral stories provide an important framework for other details, and they are an invaluable index of the values and ideas instilled in the children of the first immigrant generation.[4]

Aside from these interviews, there is little primary source material. Most of the immigrants only had a very basic education; they did not write down their experiences or impressions. They did not keep diaries or copies of the letters they sent home. Instead, they left behind store ledgers, often partially written in Arabic, and, occasionally, carefully scripted records of the birth and baptism of their children. Their business relationships were usually confined within the family and arranged without legal documentation, such as contracts, loans or wills.

Their presence, however, is notated in official documents, such as immigration and census records, applications for citizenship, city directories, license requests, and so forth. More valuable and more interesting are references in popular culture, such as in reminiscences of village life in rural New Mexico or in oblique allusions in Spanish folk tales. In addition, several transcribed interviews made as part of the Federal Writers' Project during the 1930s and 1940s provide interesting and entertaining insights into Hispanic perceptions of "los Árabes."

The chapters in this book follow both a chronological and topical order. The first chapter focuses on background information, particularly the political and economic situation in Mount Lebanon during the late nineteenth century. Especially relevant are changing economic conditions and the impact of European and American influences in the area. Specific causes for emigration are discussed in chapter two. Syrians came to the New World for the same reasons that Greeks, Italians, and many other population groups immigrated, but they also were persuaded by events that were particular to their experiences. Initially they did not plan on living in this country; they hoped to make a lot of money quickly and then return home. The arrival of the first Syrians in the territory of New Mexico is also included in chapter two.

Perhaps the most iconic description of the Syrian immigrants was of their peddling, covered in chapter three. No other immigrant group was as closely associated with this form of livelihood. It was a curious choice, because they did not customarily do this in their native country, but, like the Chinese with their laundries and the Greeks with their restaurants, the Syrians specialized exclusively in what may be loosely described as a type of service industry. Most of the first Syrians in New Mexico were peddlers; some only passed through this area, but those who stayed are the subject of this book.

Chapters four and five attempt to summarize the history and the stories of Syrian families that eventually settled in New Mexico. The quality and quantity of available information varies considerably; some families are well documented, while others only have a vague outline of past events. In spite of the risk of becoming overly genealogical, all known family names are incorporated into these two chapters. The stories include unexpected opportunities, a few hardships, as well as some unusual experiences that have enriched the history of the state. Clearly, this list is not complete; some people moved away in the early years; others died without heirs or assimilated so completely that their immigrant past has disappeared.

The assimilation of los Árabes in New Mexico is a major theme of this study. There were few, if any, cases of what are often described as painful choices of values that are a part of the immigrant experience. Since a considerable number of these immigrants were experienced cross-cultural traders, they eased effortlessly into Hispanic communities, where they encountered little if any noticeable discrimination. Chapter six details the multiple reasons for their rapid assimilation.

Hard work, a frugal lifestyle, and possibly an innate disposition toward risk-taking led a number of Syrians to various entrepreneurial enterprises, especially in the fledgling entertainment and tourism industry. Many of the names that are covered in chapter seven will be familiar to those acquainted with economic developments in New Mexico.

A study like this would be incomplete without recognizing the women who shared with their husbands the challenges of making a new home far from their families and familiar surroundings. Their spirited responses to adversity and ready accommodation to foreign customs and new surroundings are the theme of the last chapter.

This study intends to highlight the role Syrian immigrants played in the economic and cultural history of New Mexico and to identify the specific skills that helped them succeed. It is not only intended as an acknowledgment of diversity but also as an example of how the interaction of distinct cultures continues to expand and enrich our understanding of the past and of the present. In an age when immigration issues often evolve around perceived threats to cultural heritage and social order, the narrative of *Los Árabes of New Mexico* proposes a story infused with optimism, auspicious circumstances, and considerable personal fortitude.

1

Syria and Mount Lebanon in the Late Nineteenth Century

The Syrian immigrants who traveled to the New World from the end of the nineteenth century to the beginning of World War II came almost exclusively from the area encompassed by present-day Lebanon and Syria. The great majority, in fact, lived in the numerous villages of Mount Lebanon, the mountainous range that separates the slim coastal plain along the eastern Mediterranean from the agricultural valleys of the interior. In the second half of the nineteenth century this area was probably the most prosperous and densely populated area of the Ottoman Empire, a result of major political and economic developments during this period.[1]

The Ottoman Empire in 1914.

Map of modern day Lebanon.

Particularly critical was the decline of the once powerful Ottoman Empire, which was increasingly forced to rely on English and French help to sustain its territorial integrity. The European nations had entered the Crimean War of the mid-1850s to prevent the dissolution and defeat of the empire. In return the imperialist powers began to play a major role in the political, as well as economic and cultural, life of the area. Aware of its tenuous position and eager to shield its multiethnic empire from the corrosive and growing influences of nationalism and liberalism, the Istanbul government wavered between periods of extreme repression and benign neglect. Some of the empire's minorities, such as the Christians in Mount Lebanon, were accustomed to considerable self-government and so were perturbed by this political polarity.

Most importantly, these quixotic policies adversely affected the complicated relationships between the empire's many ethnic groups. Especially problematic was the situation between the Christian Maronites and the Druze, a secretive offshoot of Islam. In spite of periodic clashes, these two groups had lived together in Mount Lebanon for many generations; however, increasing tensions in the middle of the nineteenth century culminated in the 1861 Civil War that spread as far as Damascus. Although the Maronites were numerically larger and had more resources, they suffered heavy casualties and many of their villages were destroyed. Scholars differ on the number of dead, but most estimate the toll to have been around twenty thousand.[2] France and England, as the self-appointed protectors of the Christian populations in the Middle East, stepped in and proclaimed a protectorate over the Ottoman Empire's Christian subjects. This led to major changes in the area, eventually culminating in the establishment of full control by the two imperial powers after World War I with both Syria and Lebanon becoming French mandates. (Second-generation descendants often refer to the 1861 war as one of the major reasons for their parents' and relatives' emigration. Scholars, however, dispute this; emigration began twenty-five years later with another generation, while economic and political conditions improved markedly for the Christians after 1861.)

For the time being Mount Lebanon was granted a special status, called the *mutasarrifiyah*, that guaranteed the people considerable autonomy to manage their own affairs. In addition, the Christians of Mount Lebanon were exempt from military service in the Porte's armies, enjoyed a low level of taxation, and were not required to pay the traditional tribute to the sultan. (The exemption from military service was rescinded in 1908.) The sultan's government appointed a Christian official to administer this area. These privileges, along with other developments, transformed Mount Lebanon into the most prosperous area in the Ottoman Empire, a position it held until 1914.[3]

At the same time, the two European powers extended their influence and presence in other ways. They persuaded the Istanbul government to extend them specific economic privileges, which enabled them to promote the regional silk industry for the benefit of European textile mills. Thus silk was the number one industry between 1850 and 1914. This emphasis on sericulture that included the massive cultivation of mulberry trees had a major impact on the local economy. Small landholdings were consolidated and other sources of livelihood, such as olive and grape production, were curtailed. European investors set up offices in Beirut, where modern port facilities were constructed for the export of silk and the import of European manufactured goods. This concentration on a cash crop brought Lebanon into the international market. It also meant that the population was no longer self-sufficient. This had tragic consequences during World War I when residents of Mount Lebanon suffered widespread starvation.[4]

Other modernizing movements in the last quarter of the century altered the traditional isolation and inward focus of the area. The installation of telegraph lines and the construction of the first railroads marked important changes in transportation and communication. Ships' traffic followed set schedules, and the road system was expanded and improved. This was especially important for the commercial traffic between Beirut and Damascus.[5]

Aside from a growing economic presence, England and France also expanded their cultural and educational influence. Missionaries arrived to build churches and convents as well as hospitals and schools in Mount Lebanon. An influx of American Protestant missions paralleled the efforts of the British and French. An 1867 decree that permitted foreigners to hold property in the Ottoman Empire facilitated these activities.[6] It was in the educational sphere that the Europeans made a profound impact. Children, almost exclusively from Christian families, were sent to missionary schools, where they were taught not only to read and write but also English and French, European history, mathematics, and a variety of subjects that introduced them to another world outside of their immediate surroundings. (Evidently only some children attended primary school, because literacy rates of Syrian immigrants indicate that only 45-60 percent of male immigrants were literate when they arrived in America; the figures for women are much lower. Similar to other rural societies, villagers rarely appreciated the advantages of secondary education for their children.[7])

Aside from the establishment of elementary schools in some mountain villages, there were other important changes in the educational and cultural environment. In Beirut, American missionaries founded the Syrian Protestant

College in 1866; this would later become the American University.⁸ Meanwhile, French Jesuits organized the College of St. Joseph. The presence of a more literate and worldly population stimulated the publication of newspapers, journals, and other academic reviews. Unfortunately, many of the writers and intellectuals who initiated a literary revival toward the end of the nineteenth century moved to Egypt, where there was more interest in their activities and the regime was more tolerant.

Nevertheless, this new learning raised the level of expectation in the younger generation, even though much of what they learned had limited application in their lives. It also brought up questions of identity that had not been addressed previously. Several scholars in Middle Eastern history have pointed out that this new level of education alienated children enrolled in Western parochial schools because missionaries often denigrated the Ottomans while emphasizing the superiority of Europeans. Some missionaries went so far as to suggest that it was not possible to be a Christian and an Arab at the same time; their 'westernizing' attempts contributed to the confusion of identity and culture. These issues were later carried to the New World, where they became the subject of many discourses and manifested themselves in the notable absence of any allegiance or loyalty that Syrian immigrants professed for their former homeland.⁹

A growing tourist industry also contributed to the more cosmopolitan environment. Missionaries who lectured about their experiences when they returned home stimulated some of this interest in the Near East. Mark Twain visited the area in 1868; some years later Theodore Roosevelt took his son for an extended tour. Other American visitors included the Vanderbilt family and former president Ulysses S. Grant, while American ships began to include Beirut in courtesy calls in the eastern Mediterranean. These developments promoted various auxiliary industries, like accommodations, guide services, and tourist transportation that made the population more aware of the outside world.¹⁰

The increasingly larger European presence periodically alarmed the sultanate as it tried to reassert some control over its people and enforce censorship to stem the import of Western ideologies. However, these ill-fated attempts to force compliance to outmoded ideals further spurred dissatisfaction among the more educated segment of the population, while inadvertently stimulating their interest in the outside world. In summary, it was a period of rising expectations for a people interested in exploring cultural and commercial links to Europe and the New World.

Unfortunately, economic conditions began to change in the 1890s. The opening of the Suez Canal brought cheap Japanese silk to European markets. This was a major setback for what had become the most important industry in the area. Local entrepreneurs, who had come to depend on English and French merchants for work, were forced to look for other employment. This crisis was followed by an infestation of phylloxera, a plant louse that destroyed much of what was left of the grape industry. Thus a growing population, a scarcity of land, and adverse economic conditions that hindered reform and modernization promoted the idea of emigration. There were, of course, many other reasons for the exodus and these will be discussed in the next chapter.

2

Immigrating to the New World

*Y*oung men and women from the Middle East migrated to the New World for a variety of reasons—some obvious and relevant to most immigrant groups; others more complex and peculiar to the region. The publication of several memoirs, a more careful analysis of records, and some rethinking of immigration history in general have expanded this topic in recent years. Certainly the earlier focus on religious and/or political discrimination that dominated scholarship has been appraised as too narrow and simplistic.[1]

It is generally agreed that the driving force of emigration in the pre-World War I period, as well as in later years, was the promise of economic opportunity. This was especially true for those who followed family members or friends to America, from whom they heard tales of incredible wealth. A stagnant economy at the end of the nineteenth century frustrated the "rising expectations" of a people that had probably enjoyed the highest standard of living in the Ottoman Empire and reinforced the material reasons for migrations. This relative prosperity had resulted in an increase in population that put additional pressure on village communities where land resources were already scarce. Additional environmental and cultural problems in the immediate pre-war years also stimulated the idea of emigration. There was an invasion of locusts, an ongoing drought, the collapsing silk industry and an increasingly more strident and oppressive Turkish bureaucracy.[2]

Technological advances and increasing contacts with the outside world also stimulated a nascent emigration industry that included steamship agents circulating in villages, promoting travel to young men with wildly exaggerated stories about America. At the same time,

Syrian agents in European port cities simplified traveling across the Atlantic; they assisted emigrants with ship transfers and hotel accommodations while awaiting passage.[3]

Evidently it was not that difficult to convince villagers to sign up for the journey. Lebanese historian Philip Hitti mentions people who made the decision to emigrate after they saw postcards that missionaries showed them of the marvels of American cities. Many other similar stories stimulated the idea of emigration.[4] Also, travel was relatively easy; the bureaucratic constraints of visa applications, passports, and medical examinations required for departure had been suspended.[5]

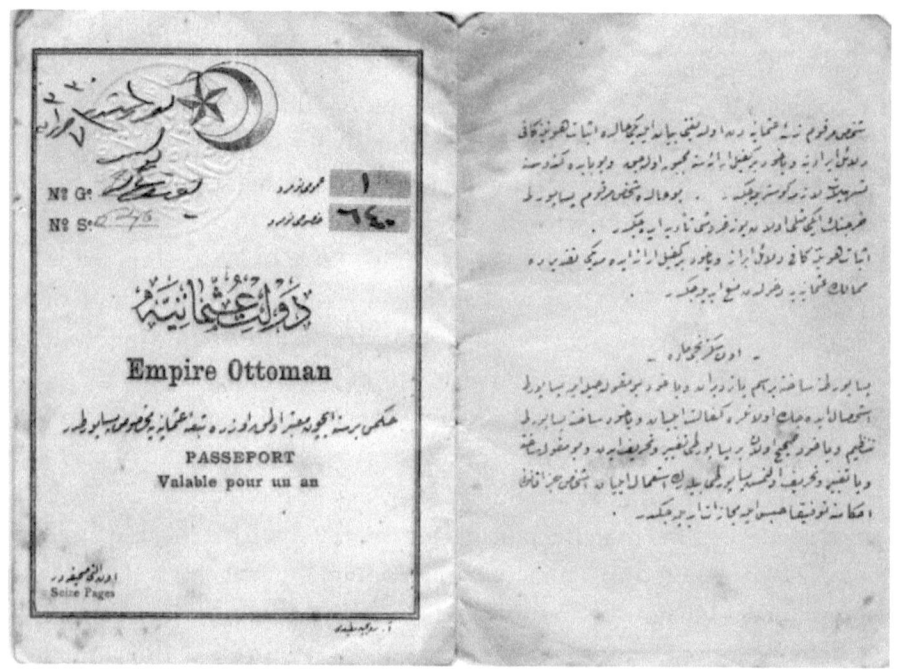

1914 Ottoman Empire passport. Courtesy Mohsen Yamine Collection, LERC.

The confining environment of village life was another factor in the exodus at the end of the nineteenth century. Memoirs and family stories often include horrendous tales of social pressures and patriarchal demands that frustrated all innovation and personal initiative. Archaic social norms included an exaggerated emphasis on family honor and the preservation of the status quo. There were disputes over land, inheritance, arranged marriages, and other age-old issues. Boys were coerced into professions they did not like and girls were put into convents or into silk factories to avoid potential problems. Individual enterprise was frowned upon, and conformity to prevailing mores was rigidly enforced. Many young men—and women—saw in America an escape from family obligations and community restrictions. One can only imagine how exciting it must have seemed to leave the tediousness and monotony of village life and journey to a foreign land.[6]

Examples of these social issues are found among Syrian immigrants in New Mexico. Elias Francis recalls that he escaped from his Syrian village during the night after an uncle had deceived him. Instead of giving him a loan, the uncle had tricked him into turning over the deed to his home. Brothers George and Joseph Abousleman say that they decided to leave and join their sister and brother-in-law in Jemez Springs, New Mexico, when their widowed father married a woman they did not like. (For their journey the father gave his sons the only negotiable item he had: a set of handmade cutlery to sell piecemeal whenever they needed money.) Rasmieh Hindi, of Duran, New Mexico, recalls thinking that going to America could be an escape from an arranged engagement to a cousin she despised. When she heard of another cousin returning from America to find a bride, she immediately agreed to marry him, sight unseen, and go with him to his new home in New Mexico. Adele Azar recounts the story of her grandmother and mother-in-law, two enterprising women who both left Mount Lebanon with several children in tow but without their husbands, reluctant to leave the comfortable security of home. LouDelle Fidel reports that in Roumieh, Mount Lebanon, the Fidel family decided that the second son, John, should study for the priesthood. More interested in business than in the church, John Fidel thought it prudent to come to America before he was sent to a seminary. Disputes over arranged marriages and quarrels over inheritances were very common reasons for leaving the country.[7]

Surely a search for adventure and independence compelled others to cross the seas and come to the New World. (A study based on a series of interviews in the Syrian immigrant community in Worcester, Massachusetts, found that "seeking adventure" was one of the primary reasons for emigrating.[8]) These young men, usually in their early twenties, were ready to see the world. Their spirit, energy, and drive often comes out of family stories, in which fathers and grandfathers are described as colorful men, risk-takers, adventurous and supremely self-confident, who continued their colorful lifestyles after they had settled permanently in their new communities.

For many years it was customary to cite religious persecution and political oppression as leading causes for the exodus that started in the late nineteenth century. Some contemporary scholars, however, contest these allegations and maintain that many of these stories are rooted in political and social issues that were current at the time. For example, Turkey, an ally of Germany in World War I, was much vilified during and immediately after World War I, and many immigrants appropriated this sentiment.

At times the Arabic press manipulated the image of oppression to address contemporary political or social problems or to solve discord within the community. Also, the American press used immigrant information to reflect its religious and/or political biases. A 1919 article in *Literary Digest*, for example, prepared "in line with education-in-Americanism," emphasized the political and religious oppression by a "Turkish Mohammadan government" of a people who were described as mountainous and of hardy stock like the people of West Virginia and Kentucky.[9]

As other immigrant groups, especially from Eastern Europe, arrived in the New World with stories of atrocities and personal exigencies, the Syrians may have found it expedient to resort to similar tales, although they as a whole were not forced out of their homeland. Many of these tales were stereotypical of general immigrant stories that focused on the many adversities that forced people to leave their homelands. Immigration studies suggest that atrocities are sometimes invoked as heritage to forge unity and enlist external sympathy.[10] In some instances the second generation, eager to assimilate and vindicate the strange speech and lifestyle of their immigrant parents, talked about oppression and persecution. In conversation, these descendants often stress the patriotism of their parents and reiterate how they had come seeking "freedom and democracy." It is most unlikely that this was the case, since these terms were not really understood at that time. Once here, of course, they relished the economic opportunities their new home offered and the freedom to pursue them.[11]

Also, the behavior of Syrian immigrants does not bear out the persecution theory. The great majority traveled to the New World with the intention of making money and then going back. In fact, the leading Arabic newspaper,

Al-Hoda, chided its readers for acting like they were on a business trip and not interested in settling down. Although the majority did stay in the United States, about 25 to 30 percent returned—one of the higher percentages among immigrant groups. (In his most recent book, *Inventing Home: Emigration, Gender, and the Middle Class in Lebanon, 1870–1920*, Akram Khater maintains that the emergence of a Lebanese middle class is directly related to these returnees.[12]) The émigrés also kept in close contact with those they left behind. In fact, emigration was often a family affair, where relatives pooled money to send someone abroad. Upon arrival, newcomers could usually expect some initial support from friends or family already here. Once established, many immigrants sent money home. Sometimes the money was earmarked for real estate investments, but more commonly to modernize the family home. These remittances made significant changes in the lives of those who stayed in Mount Lebanon. Many of the large and attractive limestone houses with red roofs, which have become emblematic of Mount Lebanon, first appeared in this period.[13]

By the early 1890s both the French consul in Mount Lebanon and Ottoman officials noted the exodus of an increasingly larger number of people. Turkish officials tried to block this phenomenon but could not decide on effective countermeasures, especially since many of the emigrants insisted that they were returning within a few years. At some point officials tried to require emigrants to post bonds ensuring their return, but this was difficult to enforce and evident bribery of officials was seemingly widespread. Moreover, some emigrants first traveled to Egypt, which was not prohibited, and then continued from there.[14]

Before concluding this part, it is necessary to point out that emigration from Mount Lebanon after World War I was very different from before the war. Those who left after World War I had suffered persecution and incredible hardships during the war. Shortly after the outbreak of hostilities, the Istanbul government canceled the special status of Mount Lebanon, and the area was put under direct Turkish control. Ottoman officials had already reinstituted the draft for Mount Lebanon in 1908, which had convinced many people to consider emigration, even though the Christian population often was able to bypass this requirement.[15] Now all able-bodied men were forcibly recruited into the Turkish armies. Some of these veterans later came to America and recounted the brutality and bitter experiences they endured during those years.

At the same time an allied blockade stopped all food shipments and monetary remittances from abroad. (The production of silk had required the conversion of arable land to the cultivation of mulberry trees. By the early 20th century the country was no longer self-sufficient and was dependent on imported food products.) The forced requisitioning of food by Turkish officials compounded this situation and a starving civilian population became susceptible to all kinds of diseases. It is generally agreed that one-quarter of the population of Mount Lebanon perished during those years due to war-related causes.[16]

In summary, the first groups of immigrants from Mount Lebanon were primarily young and single men who hoped to make some quick money and return to their homeland. Most came from small villages, where they had acquired a variety of skills, since the scarcity of land and the poor quality of the soil made full-time agriculture difficult. This adaptability to different circumstances would help them adjust to life in America. They were poor, but not destitute; Middle Eastern immigrants were not among the poorest group that arrived in Ellis Island.[17] They were not "uprooted" from their homeland, but must have been attracted by the social and economic changes taking place in the New World. Although innovative and self-assured, they had very little formal schooling; close to 50 percent were probably illiterate. Romantic notions about foreign lands led many Europeans to venture all over the globe in the nineteenth century; surely these same ideas also animated people in the Middle East.

Those who followed invariably came to join relatives, friends, and/or neighbors. Census records indicate that by the first decade of the twentieth century more than 90 percent of the immigrants came to join relatives or friends already here.[18] There are many stories of young men leaving after a letter arrived from "Amreeka" from someone familiar who had made good. Sometimes villages were depopulated virtually overnight, because a whole group of people decided to leave together after receiving some encouraging information about life overseas. In 1891, for example, a young man in the mountain village of Biskinta received a letter from his brother in America, with two hundred dollars in it. This gift electrified the whole community and forty young men left shortly thereafter. Another important impetus for leaving was the frequent return visits of earlier emigrants, who arrived in their home villages dressed in impressive Western fashions with dollars in their pockets and boasting of the incredible opportunities they had encountered.[19]

The first noticeable number of Syrian immigrants arrived in America in the mid-1880s; the National Bureau of Economic Research lists 208 immigrants in the country in 1887, the first year such records were kept.[20] Protestant missionaries in the Middle East had arranged for several students to come and study in the United States in earlier years, but these were isolated cases. There also had been several members of the clergy who had come to collect funds for their churches in the Middle East and then returned to their homeland.

Interestingly, the arrival in America of the first substantial group of Syrians can be pinpointed to a specific event in history: the 1876 Centennial International Exhibition in Philadelphia. Like many other nations, the Ottoman Empire was invited to participate in the festivities celebrating the centennial of American independence by exhibiting examples of its merchandise and cultural activities. Although the sultan requested that fair officials feature modern developments in his empire in line with the fair's theme of "progress," organizers chose instead an "orientalist" leitmotif that focused on a mysterious and exotic East—an image that was sure to appeal to attendees. And indeed it did; the Turkish exhibit was a huge success that was repeated in subsequent fairs: the 1893 World's Columbian Exposition in Chicago and the 1904 Louisiana Purchase Exposition in St. Louis. Most of the Turkish merchants who arrived in Philadelphia were Christians from Mount Lebanon. Their merchandise—that included filigree jewelry, textiles, art items, and food—sold well and they quickly realized the economic potentials in the New World. Among the most popular items were religious artifacts they marketed as coming from the Holy Land. These "sacred" items would become a popular and indispensable part of many peddlers' inventory.[21]

During the 1880s the number of immigrants from the Ottoman Empire increased slowly. Many more came in the next decade, and the numbers reached a peak in the fifteen or so years before the outbreak of World War I, when all transatlantic traffic stopped. In 1919 immigration resumed, but only for a few years. By 1921 the American government began to limit the inflow of people from eastern and southern Europe, as well as from Asia and other parts of the world. These restrictions were then formalized in the Johnson-Reed Act of 1924, which virtually ended immigration from the Middle East until after World War II.[22]

In comparison to other regions of the world, immigrants from the Middle East to the US were never a significant number in overall statistics. Most scholars estimate that about one hundred thousand people arrived before World War I and another twelve thousand between 1919 and 1924. This constitutes about 0.67 percent of total immigrants to the United States—a very small number indeed.[23] However, these figures also indicate that one-fourth of the population in Mount Lebanon had emigrated by the outbreak of World War I. One of the difficulties in calculating an exact number of Syrian immigrants is due to the fact that they were often registered under various nationalities, such as Turks, Armenians, Arabians, or Ottomans.

The United States was not the only destination in the New World. Thousands traveled to South America, especially to Brazil, as well as to Central America and Mexico. Many boarded ships in Marseille, Genoa, and other ports of departure without a specific destination in mind. Agents eager to fill a ship's quota purposely misguided some immigrants. Others were rejected at Ellis Island for health reasons and were shipped back to Beirut. Trachoma was one of the principal reasons for barring entrance into the United States. Many of those who could not enter in New York opted for immigration to other parts of the Americas; many sailed to Mexico, where entrance regulations were much less rigid; for example, trachoma was not a reason for denying entry into the country.[24]

Although many thousands of Syrians settled in Mexico, others arrived in its Atlantic ports with the intent of crossing the northern border into the United States. There must have been quite a few who chose this option, because the border patrol in El Paso hired Arabic-speaking agents as early as 1905.[25]

Theresa Alfaro-Velcamp, in her study of Middle Eastern immigrants to Mexico, included an interesting section on what could be called "an underground railroad" that operated between Mexican ports, especially Veracruz, and certain border crossing points in the north. A US immigration inspector conducted an investigation of this problem in 1906 and uncovered an operation of illegal immigrant smuggling that could be traced to Marseilles. Once immigrants arrived in the Atlantic ports, fellow countrymen would arrange temporary shelters for them and then guide them to special boarding houses in Mexico City. There they received information and advice on crossing the border: the most opportune times to enter the United States, the best way to respond to customs officials' questions, appropriate clothing to wear to avoid detection, and so forth. There were even "trachoma" doctors in the border cities who could suppress the symptoms long enough for those trying to cross at legitimate border points. The trachoma doctors customarily had English names. Immigrants were charged about twenty-five dollars for assistance with border crossings.[26]

American officials were aware of this situation but could not devise a way to stop this flow of immigrants, which also included other nationalities, especially from Eastern Europe. However, it was generally known that the Syrians constituted the largest group of these "irregular" immigrants. The correspondence of consular officials in Mexico, immigration reports, and articles in major newspapers like the *New York Times* illustrate the general concern about allowing people from the Middle East to come through "America's Back Door." Many of these objections were rooted in the negative stereotypes that were commonly used to identify Syrian immigrants.[27]

A few years later, during the turmoil of the Mexican Revolution, a number of Syrian merchants in northern Mexico crossed the border and settled in El Paso and other border areas. Entry into the United States through Mexico became especially popular in the 1920s, when the new immigration laws made it difficult to get into the United States. After residing there for a year, Syrians could cross legally into the United States. American consular officials were evidently aware of this and sent ominous reports about these practices to Washington.[28]

(In remembrance of the thousands of Middle Eastern immigrants who arrived in Veracruz, the Syrian community in Mexico erected a huge bronze statue of a Lebanese immigrant along the waterfront. With a satchel slung over his shoulders and sporting a tarboush, a fancy vest and high-laced boots, he seems to be striding inland with considerable confidence. An identical statue stands in the harbor of Beirut, but looking outward to the sea. This was a gift of the Mexican Lebanese community to their homeland.)

Mexico was the entry point for several Syrians who later settled in New Mexico. Some evidently arrived in Mexico to look up friends or relatives and then decided to continue northward; others may have come through Veracruz by mistake or because they could not enter at Ellis Island.

More than 90 percent of the Middle Eastern immigrants who came before World War I settled in the East or Midwest. They typically wanted to start out as peddlers and expected to own their own business after a few years or return home with money they had saved. Instead the majority went to work in factories, textile mills, and on the assembly line as unskilled labor. Very few settled in rural America, where their skills as farmers had little application; moreover, accustomed to living in villages, they disliked the isolation of farm life in this country.[29]

Statue of Lebanese immigrant in the harbor of Vera Cruz, Mexico. Photo by Monika Ghattas.

Their lifestyle in the East and Midwest was similar to that of immigrants from other nationalities. To cushion the impact of a strange new land, they congregated in ghettos and special neighborhoods, shopped at their own grocery stores, and preferred to work in industries that already had hired others of their ethnic background. But the most important factor in the preservation of their heritage was the establishment of churches for each of the Christian rites: Maronite, Melkite, and Antiochian Orthodox. (Very few Muslims emigrated before World War II.) Many of these appeared already by the turn of the century; here newcomers were welcomed into the community and a large variety of social, religious, and educational activities fostered a sense of belonging and continuity for the immigrants. Also important in immigrant lives was the Arabic press. There were several newspapers, each representing a different confession; among these, the Maronite-sponsored *Al-Hoda* (founded in 1892) became the most respected and prominent voice for the community nationwide.[30]

Acculturation to the American lifestyle proceeded slowly among Middle Eastern immigrants in most parts of the country. Even the second generation was slow to assimilate because both church and community fostered an internal orientation. The lure of suburban living at the end of World War II eventually weakened the cohesiveness of the ethnic community and forced a fuller participation in American life.

The first Syrians came to the territory of New Mexico in the late 1880s. (Actually a group of Syrian-Greek camel drivers came through New Mexico in the late 1850s and spent several days in the outskirts of Albuquerque. Their story is included in a later chapter.) It is improbable that any of them had selected this area as their final destination. Other than some incidental information they may have gleaned from other travelers, it is unlikely that they knew much about the territory of New Mexico before they arrived here. There is no information about the Southwest in the library of the American University of Beirut that was published before World War I. Unlike some European immigrants, the Germans, for example, there was no lore about cowboys and Indians that would have attracted them, no mystique about Native Americans or an interest in geology and anthropology. They had most likely not heard about land grants offered by the American government to settle in the far West; they probably knew nothing about the terrain or culture in this part of the country.[31]

They were peddlers traveling westward on the train, stopping at various places to sell their wares before moving on. Some journeyed to the Pacific Northwest, others to California, and a few to the Southwest. They may have heard about economic opportunities in the mines of southern Colorado, California, and Arizona, the destination of many European immigrants, especially from Italy and southeastern Europe. In some instances they stayed in an area for a while, until they had earned some money to continue westward or returned to the East or Mount Lebanon.

The most reliable sources that note the presence of "los Árabes" are found in federal census records and in New Mexico Naturalization Records that list the Declarations of Intention that immigrants were required to file in preparation for citizenship. (Immigration procedure included the following steps: obtaining a Certificate of Arrival that listed the port of entry and the carrier; filing a Declaration of Intention two years after establishing residency, which served as a declaration of allegiance to the United States and a renunciation of any other national loyalties; submitting a Petition of Naturalization five years after the first papers were filed. Many immigrants did not follow these steps.) The 1900 federal census notes Middle Eastern immigrants in several New Mexico communities. Ten years later there were 140 people from Turkey living in the territory, scattered in seventeen counties, with the majority in Bernalillo. By the beginning of World War I there were probably around 200 Syrians in the state. Colorado genealogical documents that list over fourteen hundred naturalization records for various New Mexico courts between 1882 and 1917 include several applicants with Arabic names.[32]

Listed among the first Arabs in the territory of New Mexico in the late 1880s were Moufawed Francis Hussan (later known as Elias Francis), Rasheed Michael, John D. S. El Koury, John Gabriel, and others who noted in their 1893 Declaration of Intention that they had arrived in 1888. They all came from Roumieh, a small village in Mount Lebanon, and had traveled together. Other information from records and family stories confirm that most of these early immigrants came in small groups. Moreover, they were young men, mostly in their twenties and often related; occasionally a teenager accompanied an older relative.[33]

Judith DeMark in her 1984 PhD dissertation, "The immigrant experience in Albuquerque, 1880–1920," notates the presence of Syrians in the 1890 census. She groups them together with the foreign born population from Southern and Eastern Europe. According to DeMark, one could hear many different languages in the city by the early 20th century, such as Chinese, French, and Arabic.[34]

About 50 percent of the early Syrians who settled in New Mexico emigrated from Roumieh, located about fifteen miles northeast of Beirut in the hills overlooking the Mediterranean. This became a classic model of chain migration, where relatives, friends, and neighbors followed the original emigrants for the next twenty-five years or so. This village deserves a brief description, because several descendants remembered their parents and relatives commenting about its similarity to many New Mexico communities.

Roumieh lies along the flank of mountains that rise above Beirut. Houses are scattered along the hillside with a communal spring in a central area. Olive groves, fruit orchards, and pine forests surround the village and climb upward to the next community. On a clear day one can easily see Beirut and the Mediterranean below. Even before the advent of modern roads, Roumieh was strategically located—not too far from the region's principal port in Beirut and in a transit area for those coming from villages located higher up in the mountains or from the north. Mention the words *Albuquerque* or *New Mexico* to people living there today and they will tell you immediately that this is the place where many of their people went to live. Ancestral homes in the village are still identified with these families, especially since some family members did not emigrate and continued to live there. Village store names, doctors' offices, and street signs carry names such as Saad (Sahd), Fadel (Fidel), and Younis—the same names that are found in New Mexico.

Welcome sign to Roumieh, Lebanon. Photo by Monika Ghattas.

Principal street in Roumieh, Lebanon. Photo by Monika Ghattas.

Pine forests surrounding Roumieh. Photo by Monika Ghattas.

Business sign in Roumieh with familiar name. Photo by Monika Ghattas.

Business sign in Roumieh with familiar name. Photo by Monika Ghattas.

Other Arabic names appear in early territorial records; however, census information is not always reliable. The spelling of family names often changed, and the country of origin varied in official records. Nicolas Abdalla, born in 1862 in Bishmezzine, a village in north Lebanon close to Tripoli, arrived in New Mexico in 1887—either from the East Coast or from Mexico.[35] In the last decade of the nineteenth century many more arrived in the territory of New Mexico; some of these names disappeared later on, others with Arabic names returned and eventually settled here. They include Naguib Bellamah, who came as a teenager traveling with a priest, but returned to Lebanon after a few years. The first members of the Tabet family that settled in the Manzano Mountains arrived in 1891; some of the Tabets came via Mexico. Moses Abousleman arrived in Santa Fe around 1890, and the twelfth census of the United States of 1900 lists a Simon Michael, born in 1866 in Turkey and since 1888 in New Mexico, working as a watch repairer in Gallup.

The 1910 census records Tanous Freye, Syrian, age fifty-six, living in Peña Blanca with his wife Sileby and son Alex, aged twenty-four. According to this record, he arrived in 1879, most probably a mistaken entry given the early date of arrival. There are also several men with the surname of Younis: two brothers listed as peddlers, who arrived in the early 1890s, and Regis and Rufina Younis (recorded as Unes) living with the Abousleman family in Jemez Springs. The Michael and Sahd families from Roumieh also arrived in the 1890s.[36]

In 1893 Nathan Salmon, also known as Suleiman or Solomon, traveled with a horse and wagon to Durango, but was caught with his new bride in a snowstorm outside of Santa Fe. He had to stop for a few days in the capital city and then decided to stay. The mountains reminded him of home; he would become one of the capital city's most distinguished businessmen.[37]

By the mid-1890s another group of immigrants appeared in the northern part of the state, especially around the area of Las Vegas, Wagon Mound, and Raton. Some of them had first come to the mining towns of southeast Colorado, where a substantial number of Syrians had come to peddle and later on establish stores.[38]

Interestingly, it may have been a "strong man" traveling with a circus who was the first Syrian in the territory of New Mexico. James Koury, the last second-generation descendant of the Santa Fe Koury family originally from Roumieh, reported that his grandfather, Michael David Koury (1869–1942), followed an uncle, named John Ashkar Koury, to New Mexico. The uncle had quit a traveling circus when he found a good job in the Cerrillos mines. There he befriended a Hispanic family that agreed to sponsor young Michael Koury, who arrived in the late 1880s and worked in the mines before returning to Lebanon a few years later. There he married Marie Salome Joseph (1878–1970), and they returned to New Mexico in 1901 with their oldest son, George (1899–1965), the father of interviewee James Koury. A possible explanation of the strange circus career of John Ashkar Koury may be found in Adele Younis exhaustive study of Syrian immigrants, *The Coming of the Arabic-Speaking People to the United States*, where she mentions that a number of acrobats, magicians, and other entertainers had accompanied the Turkish merchants to the 1876 Philadelphia World's Fair and then stayed in this country after they were offered work in circuses, theaters, and "Buffalo Bill Wild West Shows."[39]

The first mention of "los Árabes" in other than official records appears in the correspondence of prominent merchant and businessman Charles Ilfeld in the mid-1890s. Ilfeld and his brother-in-law, Max Nordhaus, were concerned about Arab traders in the Puerto de Luna area who were dealing in sheep and hides. They worried that the Middle Eastern peddlers were trading sheep that were in the *partido* system.[40] Ilfeld asked Hugo Goldenberg, who must have been his representative in the area, to find out the names of the Arabs. Unfortunately, there are no records of a reply. If there was a problem, it must have been amicably resolved, because shortly thereafter Ilfeld wrote to Rafael Mendes in Salada, New Mexico, that he bought 295 *borregos* (sheep) from the Arabs and would like Mendes to take care of them.[41]

Two years later, Meyer Friedman wrote to Ilfeld about renting a house in Las Vegas owned by Teodoro Casaus, a large sheep raiser in Puerto de Luna. The house was evidently rented out to a person named Maloof, and Ilfeld replied that he had been a good tenant and he did not want to evict him.[42]

~~~

In conclusion, the first Syrian peddlers arrived in New Mexico in the late 1880s via the railroad from the East or from south of the border in Mexico. They were mostly young men in their twenties who traveled in small groups and often came from the same village. Some are listed in official records, such as in naturalization and census documents; they settled in this area, while others disappeared. Most of those who decided to stay made a return trip to Mount Lebanon to bring back a wife, sometimes even a child, or to get married before coming back here permanently. In later years, usually after the turn of the century, Syrian immigrants came directly to New Mexico on the advice of relatives or friends who were already here. But even in those cases, the men customarily came by themselves; then they returned to get their families. In some cases wives followed months or even years later.

One may wonder if these Syrians differed from those who settled in the East and Midwest. Perhaps it was only a matter of chance that some came westward and decided to make New Mexico their home. It is possible that these were the more adventurous and inquisitive among immigrants who decided to venture farther west and eventually move here. Seeing some of their countrymen settle into routines of industrial and urbanized life, they may have decided to seek a lifestyle that promised more personal freedom and independence.

3

Walking Bazaars: The Peddlers

The most generic description of the Syrian immigrant was that of a peddler. As many as 90 percent of these newcomers to American life who arrived before World War I started out in this line of work, and many continued into the 1920s, 1930s, and beyond. Alixa Naff, in her seminal work on Syrian immigrants, concluded that "peddling was the most fundamental factor in the assimilation of Syrians in America."[1] Biographies and autobiographies published in recent years all include stories about the peddling experiences of early arrivals.[2] One of the more humorous recollections is that of author William P. Blatty (*The Exorcist*) who recorded the hectic years of his childhood with a peddling mother who once darted out of a waiting crowd to force a jar of quince jam on the astonished Franklin D. Roosevelt before his security detail managed to push her out of the way.[3] A sprightly peddler even made it into Rodgers and Hammerstein's *Oklahoma!*, where the wily Ali Hakim is selling egg beaters to rural housewives. The musical describes him as a Persian, while he refers to himself as a gypsy, but that character was surely based on Arab peddlers who had become quite savvy about American ways. Eastern European Jews were another ethnic group that did some peddling; however, their number was smaller, because some of these immigrants came with specific skills, like tailoring, that precluded the necessity of going on the road.[4]

This form of livelihood suited the Syrian immigrants, who preferred personal independence to wage labor; also, selling on the road required little if any training, no large capital investment, or sophisticated language skills. Moreover, it was an activity that often included the whole family; adult children and many wives also went on the road. Absent were the constraints of a fixed schedule or workplace. Surprising, too, are figures indicating that peddlers earned a pretty good living in comparison to other entry-level jobs like mining, farming, or unskilled labor. Since the great majority planned to return home after making some money in America, this line of work complemented their idea of transience.[5]

Contemporary observers had mixed feelings about these itinerant and often exotic-looking foreigners who must have been a fairly common sight in the East and Midwest. Louise Seymour Horton, one of the earliest commentators on the Syrian community, wrote a four part series on these new immigrants for *Survey* magazine in 1911. She covered a variety of topics, describing their unfamiliar food, lifestyle, clothing, and other topics. She pleaded for understanding of the peddlers and admired how they worked and lived in an unfamiliar setting. Others were not as sympathetic and insisted that peddling was a public nuisance that promoted moral laxity, deceitfulness, and a lazy disposition.[6] That peddlers had a social role in many communities, as well as an economic function, is illustrated in a popular juvenile book on that era, *The Laugh Peddler,* by Alice E. Christgau, who describes the delight of Minnesota farm wives and their children when the peddlers arrived and temporarily lifted the monotony of their lives with exciting stories and interesting merchandise, while husbands usually remained in the background, suspicious of these strangers.[7] (This mirrors the reception of peddlers in New Mexico communities that is described below.)

Almost all of the early Syrian immigrants in New Mexico started out as peddlers. Various studies on this ethnic group point out that peddling was something they had not done in their homeland, but had picked up in this country. But looking at the background of these immigrants in New Mexico, this is not quite accurate, because several came with some commercial experience, necessitated by restricted landownership and poor farming conditions on Mount Lebanon. Among these are Elias Francis, Joseph Budagher, and Nathan Salmon, as well as several families from Zahle in the Bekaa Valley, like the Hindis, Maloofs, and Azars. They had traveled in their homeland, trading regional wares to supplement their income, some going as far as Egypt, Turkey, and into the eastern Ottoman Empire. Vegetables and animals, especially sheep, were brought regularly from the Bekaa Valley to Mount Lebanon and the coast, while tropical fruit grown along the Mediterranean was transported to the mountains and the hinterland. In addition, the production of silk, a major industry until World War I, involved considerable buying and selling. This exchange of goods that included frequent bartering is not quite the same as peddling, but did involve similar skills.[8]

The great expanse of land and widely scattered population of New Mexico must have been particularly challenging to the foreign peddlers. The majority started out as foot peddlers with a pack on their back that was a type of notions box with drawers. These were called *kashshi*; in the East this term not only referred to the packs but also to the peddlers themselves. Historian Alixa Naff mentions that the name may have come from the Spanish.[9] Interestingly, Nasario García, renowned historian of the Río Puerco Valley, refers to the *cachivashes* that the Arab peddlers in the Rio Puerco area carried from one community to the next.[10] Peddlers' licenses, however, indicate that the foot peddlers with their kashshi graduated to a horse and wagon as quickly as possible. Nicolas Abdalla, for example, peddling in Socorro County, was licensed as a peddler with animal as early as 1891.[11] When Elias Francis first came to Seboyeta in the early 1890s, he had a wagon with two horses—for years locals talked about how he had arrived in the community with mismatched horses.[12] Unlike many peddlers in the East who returned to their homes either nightly or after a few days in the adjacent countryside, those in this area were often on the road for weeks and months at a time.

Jewish wholesalers outfitted many of the Syrian peddlers; this outfitting included extending credit and often providing them with a horse and wagon. Once on the road, the peddlers could request more supplies whenever stock was running low. John Amin recalled his father sending telegrams to the Ilfelds in Los Lunas about what he needed and then receiving a shipment of goods on one of the next trains. Many of these commercial relationships continued after the former peddlers established their own retail business. The young Sam Adelo accompanied his father going to Santa Fe to buy supplies from Jewish merchants and then shipping them to the family store in Pecos. Later on, established Syrian merchants helped their countrymen go on the road. According to *The Historical Encyclopedia of New Mexico*, Nathan Salmon in Santa Fe supplied more than fifty peddlers with merchandise.[13] At one point there was a Syrian wholesaler in Denver who outfitted peddlers going south to New Mexico. The Azars, Maloofs, and Hindis, who came through Colorado, received help from him. In the East, Syrian businessmen often recruited young men in Mount Lebanon with the promise of setting them up in business in

America. There is no evidence that this was done in New Mexico, where most of the later immigrants were related to those already here.[14]

Nicolas Abdalla's 1891 peddler's license. Courtesy Nick Abdalla.

The merchandise Arab peddlers in New Mexico carried was similar to that of their compatriots in other parts of the country. This included notions, ribbons, combs, clothing, kitchen items, and a variety of novelties. What was unique in New Mexico was the trade in sheep, wool, and hides. The role these items played in the local economy must have been surprising to the newcomers, since sheep and their by-products were also familiar commodities in Mount Lebanon. Surely some of these peddlers arrived with some expertise in that area and easily moved into this trade. There is no indication that peddlers in New Mexico ever carried the fine linens and Persian carpets that some peddlers in the East were later known for.

William Hindi picking up merchandise at Maloof store in Las Vegas. Courtesy Azeez Hindi.

Yet nothing identified the early Middle Eastern peddlers more than the religious items they carried in their packs. These included rosaries, pictures of saints, crucifixes, and other similar articles. Still influenced by the demand for such products at the 1876 Philadelphia World's Fair, they continued to bring this type of merchandise with them. This soon became unnecessary, because clever entrepreneurs in New York and other Eastern cities began to manufacture "genuine religious artifacts from the Holy Land" that were marketed by the peddlers.[15] Especially prized in the Southwest were little bags filled with "sacred" soil from the Holy Land. One wonders who first realized that the "holy water" peddled in the East was not a good choice in the arid Southwest and substituted the soil instead. (In some communities there was the belief that putting a little bit of "holy" dirt in the coffin of the deceased expedited their journey into heaven.[16]) These items were popular in other parts of the country, but especially among the Catholic population of New Mexico, where the demand for goods from the Holy Land never abated. Evidently Syrian peddlers in Mexico also specialized in holy relics, according to historian Theresa Alfaro-Velcamp.[17] In later years Arab peddlers focused more on household staples and groceries, but occasionally they carried some exotic items in their packs.

Interestingly, los Árabes were not the first or only group to traverse this area selling their wares from a backpack or a wagon. Marta Weigle, in her *Lore of New Mexico*, quotes Arthur L. Campa describing Hispanic *varilleros* (peddlers) who traveled with their wagons, called *ambulanzas*, throughout the state selling their goods.[18] Some early Jewish immigrants also worked as peddlers, but they were not nearly as common here as they were in the East. In his novel *The Conquest of Don Pedro*, Harvey Fergusson recounts the adventures of the fictitious Leo Mendes, a Jewish peddler traveling through central and southern New Mexico before the advent of the railroad. Like many later Syrian peddlers, Mendes eventually settled down in a village and became a respected community leader.[19]

There are also several references to gypsies traveling through this area; whether these groups were indeed gypsies or Arab peddlers is difficult to say, because both designations were often used interchangeably. (Syrian peddlers in the East often commented on being taken for gypsies.) For example, Weigle notes that some peddlers in the territorial period were gypsies known as "los turcos" or "los árabes." A letter in the Federal Writers' Project refers to gypsy troupes camped outside of towns. Since the descriptions of some of these caravans included large numbers of women and children, it is unlikely that they were Syrian peddlers who usually traveled in small groups and without their families.[20]

The confusion between gypsies and "los árabes" is also evident in William Parish's article on the nineteenth-century commercial revolution in New Mexico, titled "The German Jew and the Commercial Revolution in Territorial New Mexico, 1850–1900." He mentions that there was considerable concern during the 1890s about the influx of "árabes," whom he identified as a Middle Eastern gypsy-like people who traveled with packs on their back and traded in sheep, especially in the Puerto de Luna area, south of Las Vegas.[21]

Working on his dissertation in 1950, Parish contacted William H. Stapp in Las Vegas to ask about the matter of Arab peddlers. Stapp was evidently a descendant of the same named family that was in partnership with Ilfeld at some point. Parish quotes from the response he received in August of 1950 in which Stapp states that the term "arab" was bantered around considerably and referred to the Turkish, Syrian, and/or Arab element that did a lot of trading with ranchers in the area. They moved into the area in the late nineteenth and early twentieth century and were often referred to with opprobrium, because they had "certain gypsy tendencies." But then he added that some of these people had actually settled in the community and had done quite well.[22]

A more recent discussion on this matter appeared in a 1998 article in *La Herencia*, where Casimira Delgado recalled her mother talking about gypsies and/or turcos camped southeast of Las Vegas in the early 1900s. They traveled in wagons and peddled household goods, cloth, and other "marvelous things." They were also known as fortune-tellers.[23]

Some of the most informative accounts of Arab peddlers and their wares are found in the Federal Writers' Project, a part of the Works Progress Administration (later renamed the Work Projects Administration [WPA]). These transcribed oral history projects of the 1930s and early 1940s include information about peddlers in Hispanic villages. The interviewees describe them as "arabes" and "turcos"; the context of these stories and description of activities point to the presence of Syrian peddlers.

There is, for example, a report submitted by Lou Sage Batchen in 1941 that is based on the reminiscences of four persons from La Placita.[24] The interviewees describe two different periods when the peddlers came through La Placita—both times on the way to San Pedro, where they expected to make a lot of money. The first period supposedly was around the time of the Civil War. That would have been too early for Arab peddlers; since three of the informants were not born until after 1870 and the depositions were made in the 1930s, they probably made an error in the time. The peddlers are described as "priestly" men coming from the Holy Land who seemed like a "walking bazaar" to amazed villagers. They sometimes came barefoot into the village and then knelt to say a prayer, blessing whatever home they had been invited to enter. Most spoke some Spanish and some had tattoos of popular saints on their arms. One informant remembered the wonderful depiction of Jerusalem that one of the peddlers had on his chest. Aside from crosses, crucifixes, saints' medals, and similar objects, the peddlers also carried little bags of "holy sand" (*arenilla bendita*) that had special healing qualities. Sometimes one of the peddlers had a beautiful image of the Christ Child, wrapped in a cotton cloth. Those who were allowed to touch it were blessed or were granted a special prayer. However, before touching the image, villagers had to wash their hands seven times. In return the peddlers accepted goats, hides, and staples such as wheat. Taking into account that time may have colored their recollections, it is still obvious that the Arab peddlers were very welcome in the village; they represented a brief glance into the outside world and carried a plethora of religious items that were much in demand.

Reyes Martinez, in another WPA report, noted that a trio of Arabs visited villages in Taos County in 1890.[25] They wore "baggy trousers and tasseled fezzes, the typical garb of the races of southern Asia"; they played music on inflatable instruments and had a black bear on a chain that collected money from the bystanders. These stories, of course, must be evaluated in light of the fact that more than forty years had passed since these events had occurred. In another report a Persian women had left her band of peddlers to marry a man from Ranchitos.[26]

Nasario García remembers Arab vendors who came into the area when he was young. They wore shiny shirts and had a great variety of goods for sale or trade. One of Garcia's most recent books, *The Naked Rainbow and Other Stories*, includes the tale of a peddler, who is "painted" by village women after he sold them a salve that gave them a rash. Although the account is fictitious, Garcia alludes to village impressions of these itinerant salesmen, who sometimes took advantage of the easy gullibility of the people. It is clear that the peddlers were regulars in village life, often passing through when the people were more likely to have some money—after the harvest or during fiesta time, like St. John's Day on June 24. In this tale the peddler is called Abdul Habib, a common Arab name, who along with perfumes and creams carried a ceramic crèche that was much admired. The villagers assume he is one of the Arab peddlers, but in the end it turns out that he is "a gypsy, a turco, as they were called long ago in northern New Mexico."[27]

Another ambivalent view of Arab peddlers comes from a 1951 article in *New Mexico Magazine*, titled "Peddlers in the Old Frontier." Author K. D. Stoes reiterated the colorful role of peddlers in territorial New Mexico. They came from the "outside world" and brought all kinds of exciting news: stories of adventure, encounters with Apaches and outlaws, getting lost in the wilderness, new fashions, and so forth. The only other occasional visitor was a clergyman, who was not nearly as popular. Work in the village came to a halt as these colorful visitors were invited for dinner and given a bed for the night. The peddlers carried religious items and statues for the *nichos*; however, as the writer recalled, "once a 'wily Syrian' tried to substitute a strange statue for our own San Albino, patron saint of La Mesilla. We were all too well acquainted with our own Santo to permit such chicanery."[28]

The vivid impressions these foreign peddlers left in some of the communities through which they passed can be measured by their inclusion in Hispanic folktales, like the story of "El camello que se perdió," which begins like this: "There were once some merchants from across the ocean who traveled from place to place selling their wares. Late one evening as they made their way up the Rio Grande they lost one of their camels."[29] Embellishing this tale with an exotic animal adds to the charm and mystery of this story. However, the inclusion of a camel in this Spanish folktale does have a basis in actual events. In the 1850s, Secretary of War Jefferson Davis arranged for the import of camels to be used in the American Southwest for carrying goods in a desert climate. About seventy-seven camels eventually were brought to this country, and a Syrian by the name of Hadji Ali was put in charge of their trek across the Southwest. The whole project lasted only a few years, but the story of the US Camel Corps has become an entertaining sideline in Southwest history.[30]

In August 1857, Lieutenant Edward Fitzgerald Beale brought the Camel Corps up the Rio Grande Valley on his way to Fort Defiance, from where he was supposed to survey a wagon/camel route to Fort Tejon in California. He stopped a couple of days in Albuquerque, where the drovers and camels quartered, while Beale traveled to Santa Fe to report to the commanding officer. When he returned, he found that Hadji Ali and the other drovers, who included Greek George and another Turk, "had succumbed to the temptations of the flesh" and were drunk. But Beale could not let them go; he was dependent on the expertise of the drovers and continued with them to California. Hadji Ali, later more commonly known as Hi Jolly, became a colorful character who spent most of his life in Arizona where he died in 1902; his life is commemorated in an annual fiesta in Quartzite, Arizona.

Another Turkish camel drover, named Elias, evidently returned to Texas, but moved to New Mexico in the 1860s. Some time later he moved to Sonora, Mexico, where Hi Jolly also lived for a while. In the 1920s a woman from New Mexico visited the president of Mexico, Plutarco Elias Calles, at Chapultepec Castle. He regaled her with his father's stories of driving camels up the Rio Grande Valley and his time in New Mexico. According to the president, his father had been a well-known character in the Southwest in the 1860s. After he arrived in Sonora, he married a Yaqui Indian girl and fathered the future president. Elias Calles was known as 'el turco' in Mexican political circles.[31]

In the East and Midwest it was not uncommon to see female peddlers; in fact, it was generally felt that women were more successful as peddlers, because they had an easier access to other women, both in the suburbs and in the countryside. The issue of women peddlers became a disputed topic in the Arabic press.[32] It certainly was a breach in tradition, but women enjoyed this unexpected freedom. There are quite a few stories of married women who came to America specifically to earn money as peddlers. Both the grandmother and mother-in-law of Adele Azar came to Colorado to peddle. They brought their older children with them but left their husbands back in Mount Lebanon. In southern Colorado they stayed with brothers and peddled in the mining camps around Trinidad. Some of the Azars later moved south to Clayton. There is also mention of a Syrian woman who came out of El Paso and traded among the Mescalero Indians in southern New Mexico. She made a fortune, so the story goes, and eventually returned to Mount Lebanon.[33] In New Mexico there is no evidence of Syrian women selling from door to door, except for Clara Sahd, who was forced to go on the road after her husband died in the 1930s. Her story is included in a later section.

Unfortunately, most of the peddling stories of the first-generation immigrants in New Mexico have been lost. There are, however, a couple of accounts that have survived and illustrate the plethora of experiences these people encountered. One of these tales comes from the Sahd family. Abdo Youssef Saad (the original family name) arrived here in the late 1880s, the first member of a large family that settled in New Mexico. Together with a few relatives he peddled with horse and wagon through much of northern and central New Mexico. But he missed his wife and two small sons whom he had left behind in Mount Lebanon. So he sent a letter to his wife with one of his returning countrymen, asking her to send him a family photo that had been taken just before Saad's departure. But he returned home in 1898 before the photo arrived. Like so many others, he made a second trip to the New

World and to New Mexico a few years later. This time he brought his older son, Butros Abdo (later known as Peter A. or Don Pedro) with him. They first sailed to Columbia to stay with relatives, then left for Mexico because of a looming political crisis. Similar problems in Mexico convinced Saad to return to New Mexico, where he worked in Albuquerque and Cerrillos. In 1908 father and son returned to Mount Lebanon so that Peter could get married. After World War I, the younger Sahd, now married and with a couple of children, immigrated to New Mexico, where he had been as a young boy with his father. Eventually he established a mercantile business in Taos, but he also continued to peddle in the Hispanic villages of northern New Mexico. One evening he was invited to stay overnight with a family in Rociada, a customary gesture in rural New Mexico. While the lady of the house went into the kitchen to get him something to eat, Sahd looked around the room and was intrigued by a picture in a bronze colored frame, prominently displayed with other religious items in the family's *nicho*. He went over to look at it more carefully. When the woman returned from the kitchen she proudly explained that they had acquired this portrait of the Holy Family from an Arab peddler years ago. She went on to tell her astonished guest that this family treasure depicted Mary and Joseph with the Baby Jesus and Saint John. Sahd, who had immediately recognized the lost family portrait, decided to leave things as they were and not destroy the symbolic value of the photo.[34]

Elias Francis was also one of the earliest Syrian peddlers in New Mexico. He traveled westward on the train and a couple of his peddling experiences are part of the family history. To save money he customarily spent the night in the train depot, but in Topeka the stationmaster refused to let him do so and directed him to a nearby hotel instead. Francis realized that he did not have enough money to pay for his room and would have to sell some merchandise quickly. So he pulled out some of the traditional Arabic clothes that he had kept at the bottom of his pack. These included a tarboosh, the typical baggy *sharwal*-style pants worn in Mount Lebanon, and an embroidered vest to which he added several strings of beads and medallions. Playing the role of a holy man, he went downstairs and entered the hotel dining room, where he offered the astonished patrons a wide array of "blessed relics" from the Holy Land. He sold everything in no time at all and the hotel manager, grateful for the free publicity, did not charge him for the room. In later years he told his family that he made a vow that henceforth he would only stay in first-class hotels.[35]

His grandson, E. Lee Francis II, recounted another incident when his peddling grandfather fled Tierra Amarilla during the middle of the night, because he heard a rumor that some people were going to rob him. Clearly amused, the former lieutenant governor added that he remembered that incident when he called out the New Mexico National Guard to put down the Reies López Tijerina courthouse raid in 1967.[36]

Like their countrymen in other parts of the United States, the Syrian peddlers in New Mexico were resourceful, self-sufficient, and very tenacious in the pursuit of their objective: economic success. They traveled through a strange land, often under very taxing circumstances, but quickly learned to market their goods with much ingenuity, wit, and good humor.[37] In spite of their occasional dubious sales techniques, they were generally welcome in the communities through which they passed. For example, years later villagers in the Rio Puerco Valley remembered the Arab peddlers from Albuquerque with their fresh fruit and vegetables.[38] Fuad Amin often talked to his children about his peddling days in the Estancia Valley and along the Rio Grande corridor south of Socorro. On Saturday night, local cowboys and ranch hands would give him their extra cash for safekeeping while they went into town.[39] Similar welcoming experiences come from other stories of the early pioneer families, like the Budagher, Adelo, and Abousleman families.

Several Syrians continued to peddle after World War I, even though they had established a permanent business. Their inventory usually came from their stores and often included groceries; over the years more and more traveled in cars and trucks instead of in wagons. Surely some of the Syrian merchants peddled to augment their income, but others continued because they enjoyed the freedom and flexibility of this lifestyle.

Although not seen as such at the time, peddling was a form of cultural immersion that proved to be quite successful. These itinerant merchants were forced to make immediate contact with a different culture and to learn some essential vocabulary. For those who came to the Southwest, peddling was a unique introduction to the lifestyle and geography of this area. Evidently even those who returned to Lebanon permanently were transformed by ideas and practices they had experienced on the road in America and would become the fulcrum of gradual village modernization.

4

From Sojourners to Settlers

By the mid-1890s several Syrian peddlers had saved enough money to establish a permanent business in New Mexico. The great majority chose small Hispanic villages or newly founded railroad and mining towns as business locations. Very few worked directly for the railroad or in the mines, but, well aware of the economic potential in these communities, they focused on auxiliary services, such as food, clothing, and other necessities. Some of these immigrants who came from Zahle in the Bekaa Valley and settled primarily in the northern part of the state were familiar with the economic impact of railroads. Zahle was a major stop on the narrow gauge line that was completed in 1895 between Beirut and Damascus. Unlike their countrymen in other parts of the United States, only a few families initially settled in the semi-urban environments of Santa Fe, Las Vegas, and Albuquerque.[1]

Operating a general store insured the personal independence prized by Syrian immigrants and also met their goal of self-employment. This form of livelihood supported the immediate family as well as relatives and friends who followed later. Newcomers could expect a job or the seed stock to enable them to go on the road as peddlers. After a few years of traveling, they would have identified another community that was suitable for opening their own business. There was an informal agreement among them that newcomers would set up a new business in a community that did not already have a Syrian merchant. Also, Hispanic villagers traditionally preferred farming to commercial activities and thus did not resent their presence.[2]

By the mid-1920s there were Syrian-owned general stores in many New Mexico communities—in the central corridor from Belen to Las Cruces, including Socorro, Truth or Consequences, San Macial, and Magdalena; in the north there were mercantile businesses in Raton, Wagon Mound, Springer, and Clayton, as well as several in Taos and in San Miguel County. And there were stores in the central and eastern areas of the state, such as in Duran, Santa Rosa, Carrizozo, and in Cibola County and other points west. In addition, Syrians were engaged in a variety of business ventures in Santa Fe, Albuquerque, Bernalillo, and Las Vegas. Ted Sahd, an Albuquerque resident and the descendant of one of the larger Syrian families, remembered that there was a time after World War II when he had a relative in practically every community in northern New Mexico.[3]

Apart from operating general stores, several Syrian families expanded into the traditional New Mexico livelihoods of sheep and cattle raising. As ranchers they employed workers from the surrounding communities and shipped stock nationwide. Their economic impact in this state belies their relatively small number.

This chapter and the following impart histories of some of the Syrian families that settled in different parts of the state. This is not an inclusive study; for some families there is very little information available, and for others, information has seemingly disappeared. The first part will focus on the Syrian families who settled in the Rio Abajo area and in the western parts of the state. Those who moved into the communities of central and northern New Mexico will be covered in the following chapter.

***

The first members of the large Tabet family arrived in New Mexico in the early 1890s.[4] They came from Bhamdoun, a small town in Mount Lebanon, landed in Veracruz, and then traveled northward to cross the border at El Paso. The 1900 census lists three brothers living in Lincoln, New Mexico: Tannous (b. 1870), Carlos (b. 1872), and Abraham (b. 1880).[5] All were identified as single and as merchants. (Descendants are not sure whether the three men were brothers or cousins. A fourth relative, Nassif Tabet, appears in subsequent records, but there is no further mention of Abraham Tabet, who may have returned or gone elsewhere.) According to a 1937 study of Manzano, Tannous Tabet arrived there in 1902; various relatives followed him and settled in Mountainair, Manzano, Torreon, Chilili, Pinos Wells, and Punta de Agua, a railroad boomtown in those years.[6] At one point there were four Tabet families living within a block of one another in Mountainair; these included

Juan (b. 1889) and Farida Tabet, who arrived in New Mexico in 1907. Juan's original name was Akel Tabet, but he was promptly renamed "Juan" because he arrived in Mountainair on St. John's Day.[7]

Tabet sisters in Mountainair, New Mexico. Courtesy Viola Sanchez.

Another set of brothers and a sister had arrived in 1905. They include Elias Tabet and his wife Anisa, both born in Bhamdoun, who landed in Veracruz and legally entered the United States at El Paso in 1905.[8] Their travels can be followed through the birth of their eleven children: the two oldest were born in Mount Lebanon, the third in Chilili, the fourth in Torreon, and the rest in Manzano. Another brother, Khalil, born in 1870 and listed alternately as Calixo or Kalistro, married the much younger Severa Gonzales (b. 1890). According to their descendants, she became completely "syrianized"; she learned Arabic and cooked only Middle Eastern food. Most of their nine children were born in Punta de Agua; many moved to southern California in later years. (When their son, Samuel K. Sr., died in the spring of 2012, grandson, Samuel K. Tabet, Jr., spoke at the funeral about his father's youth in Mountainair, where he was known as "el Arabito"—the little Arab.)[9]

There are thirty Tabets listed in the 1920 census; obviously, some were children. Tannous Tabet is counted twice, once under his proper name and another time as George Labat from Syria in Turkey. The 1920 census is a good example of variations in official listings. The birthplace of the different Tabets is noted alternately as the Syrian Arab Republic, Turkey, and Arabia; curiously, several Tabets are marked as Native American Indians in the race category.[10]

One of the best sources for the Tabet families is a book published in the 1980s by Wesley R. Hurt on the Manzano Mountain area. The study is based on the author's master's thesis written in 1935.[11] Noted here is the arrival of Tannous Tabet in the early 1890s, peddling with his "brothers" in the area. He went back to Mount Lebanon a few years later to get his wife and returned to Manzano in 1902 with a wagon full of supplies that he had purchased in Albuquerque. His store did not do very well the first year, and he was planning to return to Albuquerque when he learned that the railroad was extending its line through Abo Pass and needed one and a half million railroad ties. This brought lumber people into the Manzano area, and Tabet earned more than $10,000 the next year. The local economy boomed and so did Tabet, who, with the largest store in the area, periodically dispatched twenty-five to thirty wagons to Albuquerque, loaded with pelts, wool, and hides to be exchanged for supplies. During one of the local fiestas, Tabet earned $700 in one day; on the same day an unknown Syrian peddler put up a stand in front of his store and made an additional $400. Tabet also invested in sheep and was listed as one of the largest sheep owners in the area. In the early 1900s he opened a store for a cousin in Punta de Agua.[12] Hurt's report states that the traditional peon/patron system was strengthened in the area; Anglo lumber company officials and Arab merchants were the new "patrones," who provided employment, advice, and economic opportunities to the community.[13]

In 1905 the territory of New Mexico put a claim against the Manzano Land Grant for $1,600 in back taxes. The Land Grant Commissioners asked Tabet to pay the bill, because the community could not come up with the money. Over the next few years he collected the money in small increments from the people and nearly recovered the full amount. In 1912 Tabet sold out to his sons and moved to the newly founded town of Mountainair.[14] In the meantime, his brother (or cousin), Carlos, had married the fifteen-year-old Onesima Garcia from Los Trujillos. They operated a saloon and store in Punta de Agua, but eventually settled in Belen, where several of their descendants still live.[15] A population study in 1939 indicates that there were still five Syrians living in Manzano, along with eleven Anglos. Some of the Tabets moved to California, but there are still many family members in Belen, Los Lunas, and Albuquerque.[16]

Carlos and Onesima Garcia Tabet with children. Courtesy Viola Sanchez.

In Belen, Carlos Tabet Sr. operated a variety of businesses that included grocery stores, a bar, a beer bottling plant, and Tabet Hall, the popular site of many local weddings and dances. He did not speak English, but he could make himself understood in Spanish. His family remembered the federal agents from Albuquerque who visited him a couple of times during World War II because he refused to observe the ration card allotments. When he could not answer in English on the agents' first formal visit, they sent a Spanish-speaking agent. He returned to the office and reported that Tabet did not speak Spanish either and they had to let the matter go. Before he died, Carlos Tabet told his children that he wanted all customer debts on the books forgiven upon his death. When his children tried to see how much money was outstanding after he died, they discovered that Tabet had notated everything in Arabic, which they could not decipher.[17]

Carlos Tabet. Courtesy Viola Sanchez.

The Hindis were another large and prominent Syrian family that settled east of the Manzano Mountains in the Estancia Valley.[18] They came from Zahle, an important commercial center in the Bekaa valley, east of Mount Lebanon.

Like their friends, the Maloof and Fram families of the same hometown, brothers Milhelm and Ali Hindi had been traders, shipping goods between Damascus and Beirut. In the early 1900s they decided to move to Las Vegas, New Mexico, where they were outfitted with horse and wagon to peddle in the area. Several years later a nephew, Kassem Hindi, and a younger brother, Amin, joined William and Alex, the Anglicized names they would become known by.[19]

Alec and William Hindi with nephew Kassim. Courtesy Brahaim Hindi, Jr.

Their peddling eventually led them to Duran, New Mexico, then a typical railroad boomtown with a roundhouse for locomotive repairs, plus attendant hotels, saloons, and restaurants for the burgeoning population, which reached three thousand inhabitants at one point. (Today Duran has thirty residents at most.) It was an ideal place to settle down and start a business.

Vacant Hindi store in Duran, New Mexico. Photo by Monika Ghattas.

Stone marker to Hindi Ranch in Duran, New Mexico. Photo by Monika Ghattas.

Alex Hindi was the first to marry, in 1916. His wife, Clarita Duran, belonged to a Basque family that had come from Spain in the late 1800s. William Hindi, on the other hand, returned to Lebanon at the end of World War I to marry his cousin, Razmieh Hindi. Both brothers had large families; unlike other families from Mount Lebanon, their children were given typical Arabic names, such as Brahaim, Samira, Farisa, Nabai, and Moneer.

William and Razmie Hindi with children. Courtesy Brahaim Hindi, Jr.

Alex and Clarita Duran Hindi.
Courtesy Brahaim Hindi, Jr.

Brahaim Hindi, Sr. in 2011.
Photo by Monika Ghattas.

The Hindi brothers opened a retail business in Duran and expanded into ranching shortly thereafter. After a few years, they decided to separate their business interests; William focused on the general store in town, which was located along the railroad tracks. This building, abandoned years ago, still stands in the same place with the name of William Hindi clearly visible. Alex Hindi built a huge sheep and cattle business; at one point he controlled 200,000 acres of land with tens of thousands of sheep. Some of this acreage came from failed homestead claims that he bought. After World War II, he made a visit to Lebanon and arranged for Arabian racehorses to be shipped to New Mexico. Thus the family became famous as breeders of Arabian horses, which were shown in many parts of the country and annually at the New Mexico State Fair. On the walls of grandson Brahaim Hindi's house in Duran are pictures of these prized horses, including the original ones shipped from Beirut in the 1940s.[20]

All the Hindi children grew up speaking Spanish and Arabic; after primary school they were sent on the train to Santa Fe boarding schools. Alex's wife, Clarita Duran, became fluent in the language of her husband. The special dialect and forms of expression that are associated with the people of Zahle in modern-day Lebanon are still noticeable today in the third generation.

Graves of William and Alex Hindi in Duran, New Mexico. Photo by Monika Ghattas.

Interestingly, there was another Syrian family in Duran that also had a dry goods store by the tracks, but this family is remembered for other reasons. Anton Coury must have peddled in New Mexico and Arizona in the late1890s, before he returned to Mount Lebanon to marry his childhood sweetheart, Rafnaa Elias (1882–1968).[21] After returning to America, they spent some time in Arizona, but then moved to Santa Rosa, where Anton's brother, Gabriel Coury, and family had settled. In 1913, Anton Coury bought the Kilmer mercantile business in Duran. Unfortunately, the store burned to the ground in 1917, but the Courys rebuilt and added their living quarters above, plus thirteen rooms for boarders.[22] (The building is still standing in Duran.) In September 1921, shortly after closing, two outlaws entered the store, demanded money, and killed Anton Coury as he bent over a pickle barrel. They also shot his wife; fortunately, she survived. The first bullet ricocheted off her corset, and then one of the robbers' gun jammed as the Courys' son began hurling cans of tomatoes at the men. The robbers fled on their horses together with three accomplices waiting outside. Four of the outlaws were eventually captured and brought to trial in Estancia. Rafnaa Coury testified at the trial and all four were hung—it was the last legal hanging in the state of New Mexico.[23] Coury's nephew, Raymond Shaya, believed that this crime was a revenge crime; Anton Coury had been a deputy sheriff in Santa Rosa and had arrested five of the outlaws for cattle rustling.

Coury store in Duran, New Mexico, 1920. Courtesy Carole Darr.

Vacant Coury store in Duran, New Mexico in 2010. Photo by Monika Ghattas.

Coury store advertisement. Photo by Monika Ghattas.

The 1920 US census records twenty-three people with the surname of Salome living in Socorro County, members of an extended family whose residences and businesses stretched from Socorro to El Paso and included Belen, Carrizozo, and Santa Rosa.²⁴ The most picturesque reminder of this family is in Magdalena, where the Salome country store was placed on the National Register of Historic places in 1982. With its embossed tin ceiling tiles and creaky wooden floor, an antique wooden bench for trying on boots and a glass case for storing wedding gowns, the store still conjures a certain nostalgic link to the days when groceries, animal feed, blankets, clothing, and Navajo jewelry were for sale here.²⁵ Brothers George (b. 1865) and Joe Salome (b. 1880) built the store in 1910 with money George's wife, Ida, received as compensation from a railroad accident. The Salomes had come from Oklahoma and had peddled in the area for about ten years.

Salome store in Magdalena, New Mexico. Photo by Monika Ghattas.

Magdalena was a good choice for settling down; the town had been established in 1894 and was a major mining and livestock center—probably the most important commercial community in west-central New Mexico. Magdalena's spur line from Socorro was the most profitable thirty miles on the

Atchison, Topeka and Santa Fe Railway. Cattle arrived from eastern Arizona and western New Mexico to be shipped out of Magdalena, while lead, zinc, and silver were mined in nearby mountains.[26]

Magdalena flourished until the 1930s, when the Depression, the arrival of the trucking industry, and the area's depleted ores brought an end to the town's prosperity. However, the Salome store continued; it had become not only important in the community but also was a stopping place for ranchers and cowboys from the surrounding countryside, for the Navajos from the nearby Alamo Reservation, and from the remaining miners from Kelly.

According to the Salomes' granddaughters, Jill Salome and Jeanette Salome Atencio, the grandparents spoke Arabic and Spanish at home with their four children. Jill described her grandfather as a "character" well known in the community for his uninhibited behavior. Her father, Morgan (1907–1987), who took over the store after George Salome died, was also recognized for his independent streak; in the 1940s he killed a cowboy in a saloon by breaking a bottle over his head. Conflicting testimony from the witnesses resulted in his acquittal.

Three nephews followed their uncles to Magdalena; one of the brothers, Fred Salome (1887–1962), had worked for the railroad in Torrance County and Santa Fe. He returned to Lebanon in 1911 to get married, but was back in Magdalena a year later, where he opened a bakery and pool hall. His older daughter, Clara Salome Fidel, was born there. In 1914 he moved his family to San Macial, a thriving railroad town along the Rio Grande with a roundhouse and a Fred Harvey hotel. There he operated a general merchandise store until 1929, when a flood swept San Macial away. Later Salome bought land in the Mesilla Valley, where he grew cotton and alfalfa, plus Syrian vegetables and exceptional apricots.[27] One of Fred Salome's brothers also lost a business in San Macial and eventually moved to El Paso, while the youngest brother lived in Socorro and later in Las Cruces. Clara Salome Fidel recalled that there was also a Salome cousin in Santa Rosa, as well as her mother's relatives, one of the many Koury families in the state.

Clara Salome Fidel remembered her father as a storyteller, who had brought books of poetry and fables from his home in Mount Lebanon. During her youth there was much socializing with relatives in Magdalena and also with the Syrians in Cibola County. Often the family traveled by horse and wagon and then spent several days visiting or celebrating a family event.

These occasions customarily included Middle Eastern music and lots of dancing, including improvised sword dances with kitchen knives. After Clara Salome Fidel's mother died in 1918, her father remarried the daughter of a prominent West Texas ranching family. This connection brought the family into the Anglo community, and Salome joined various civic organizations and the Masons.

Among other Syrian immigrants in the Rio Abajo area was Nicolas Abdalla (1862–1937), who arrived in the late 1880s from northern Lebanon where his family was in the silk business.[28] Family lore tells that he came to the New World as a stowaway, but it is not clear whether he came through Ellis Island or Mexico. He peddled south of Socorro for several years and then married Marianita Chavez from Lemitar, whose father had some property in the area and a general store. Abdalla managed his father-in-law's business and eventually inherited it when Chavez died. The couple had ten children; the father meticulously recorded the details of their births in Arabic script.[29]

Wedding portrait of Nicolas Abdalla and Marianita Chavez. Courtesy Nick Abdalla.

In an undated letter, most likely written some years after Abdalla's death, his son-in-law, Charlie (no last name), the husband of daughter Katherine, summarized Abdalla's experiences. It is not clear to whom he was writing, but he was evidently responding to someone who knew the family well in earlier years. The correspondent relates Abdalla's arrival in New Mexico and how he built a large store that he ran for over forty years. Also mentioned in the letter are Abdalla's efforts in bringing three nephews to New Mexico. Their surnames are noted as Goze, Shahin, and Koury. George Goze is detailed below and Mikhael Shaheen (a.k.a. Mikhael Chahin) appears in Socorro County records, where he is listed as a merchant who sailed from Tripoli, Lebanon, to Veracruz, Mexico, arriving in Magdalena, New Mexico, in 1913. Koury is more difficult to trace, because there were several Syrian families with that surname.[30]

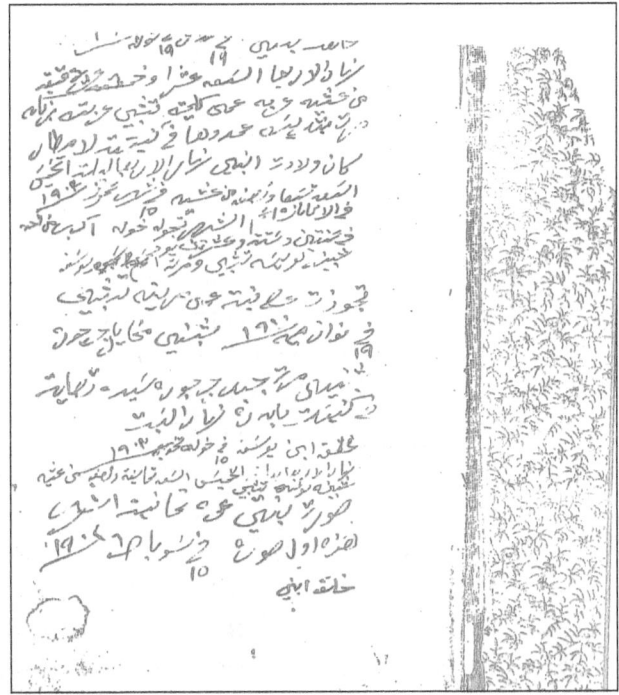

Nicolas Abdalla marking the birth of his children. Courtesy Nick Abdalla.

Probably sponsored by his uncle, Nicolas Abdalla, George Goze (1886–1948) came directly to Albuquerque in 1907. After working in the railroad shops for a short period, he bought a horse and wagon and peddled beans, pelts, and hides in central and southern New Mexico. In 1916 he settled in Magdalena and opened a general merchandise store across the street from the Salome business. Within a few years he went into the sheep and cattle business and became one of the most important ranchers in the area. With land in Mendoza and Rosa Canyon, he raised Hereford bulls and grew his own feed.

The Goze family also owned the wool warehouse in Magdalena. George Goze was a member of the Cattle Growers Association for many years and served on the Socorro County Commission.[31]

Today the Amin name is associated with a furniture and clothing store in Truth or Consequences. Fred Amin (1892–1978), who previously had peddled and worked in the area for over twenty years, established the business in the early 1930s.[32] The sixteen year old Amin, whose original name was Fuad Ameen, arrived on Ellis Island in 1908 from Roumieh. Related to several other families already in New Mexico, Amin first came to Albuquerque, where an uncle, K. Koury, owner of a clothing store on Central Avenue, outfitted him with a horse and wagon. He peddled in the Estancia Valley, Silver City, the Gila Wilderness, and in a number of now almost forgotten railroad towns, like Monticello, Cutter, and Engle, New Mexico. The congenial Amin made a lot of friends on his travels, especially among the cowboys and ranchers. But life was not easy. In later years he recounted the bitterly cold winters on the plains when he had to bury himself in snowbanks to keep warm.

His first general merchandise store in Willard burned down; when an area rancher offered to put him back in business if he married his daughter, Amin decided it was time to move on. His next venture was a vegetable market in Holbrook, Arizona. However, World War I broke out and he enlisted in the army and was sent to France. By the time he returned in 1918, his business had gone bankrupt. Disappointed, he decided that this was a perfect time to go home and get married. A few years later he briefly returned to Holbrook with his family, which included his wife, Labibe Merhige (b. 1906), whose brothers had settled in Española, and Joseph, the oldest of his eight children. Since business in Arizona was not very encouraging, Amin came back to New Mexico and finally settled in Truth or Consequences. His brother John, who spent a few years in the area, eventually returned to Lebanon. Four of the five Amin sons served in World War II.

Also residing in Truth or Consequences in the late 1930s was Zaid Fandey and his family. Fandey left Lebanon before World War I and lived in Texas and Missouri, working as a peddler and doing odd jobs before coming to Hobbs, where he lived for about eight years. Bad luck with a restaurant business convinced him to make a new start in another community. A second attempt to go into the food business did not succeed, and Fandey eventually built a large sporting goods store in Truth or Consequences.[33]

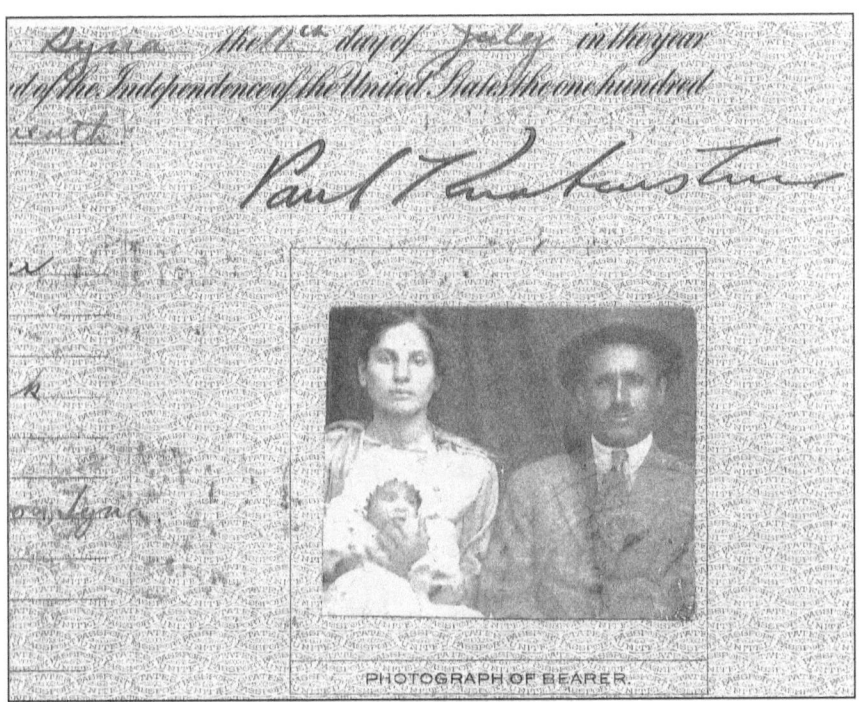
1922 passport photo of Fred Amin, wife Labibi, and son Youssef. Courtesy John Amin.

John Amin in Truth or Consequences, New Mexico, 2009. Photo by Monika Ghattas.

Zaid Fandey and sons, 1940. Courtesy Fayze Fandey.

Some of New Mexico's most prominent families who came from Mount Lebanon settled west of Albuquerque in Seboyeta, Grants, San Mateo, Bibo, Cubero, and other small communities in Cibola County. They include the Francis, Hanosh, Michael, and Fidel families, all from Roumieh in Mount Lebanon and all related in multiple ways. Several of the descendants have been involved in state politics and are still engaged in various commercial activities in the area; their stories are well documented. In recognition of their role in the history of Cibola County, New Mexico historian Abe Peña included a chapter on the Lebanese immigrants in his book *Memories of Cibola*.[34] There were also a few other families in the area, like Assad and Wardie Harp in San

Mateo and a Koury family in Gallup, but there is very little information on them.

Judging by his Declaration of Intention filed in 1893, Elias Francis (1858–1930) was one of the first Syrians to come to New Mexico, in 1888.[35] He returned to Mount Lebanon a few years later to get his wife, Pauline Hanosh (1858–1946), and son, Nasif, known as Narciso Francis. After working a short time in Albuquerque, he decided to move to the old fortress town of Seboyeta, because it promised more economic opportunities and reminded him of Mount Lebanon. It must have been some earlier peddling that had led Francis into the area of Seboyeta, then known as Cebolleta. Little of what remains in Seboyeta today is testimony to its colorful and turbulent history. Founded as a frontier community with walls and watchtowers, it had become a major center of the sheep industry by the late nineteenth century and also lay close to the recently completed east-west railroad. Close by were a couple of Indian pueblos and the Navajo reservation. As a thriving and growing community, Seboyeta stimulated the founding of several other communities in the area, such as Grants, San Mateo, Cubero, and San Rafael.[36] Originally known as Cebolleta, the town had to select another name when it applied for a post office, because it sounded too similar to Cebolla, New Mexico. (Narciso Francis applied for the post office and selected the new name for the community. Once it was granted, he became the first postmaster general.[37])

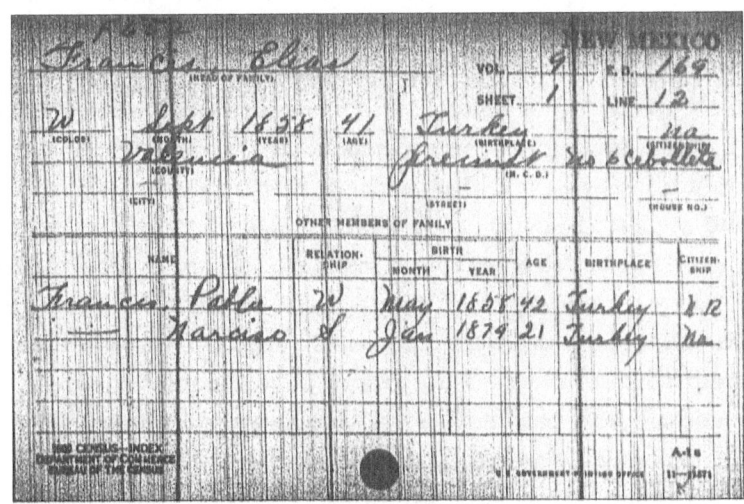

1900 census listing Francis family from Turkey living in Cebolleta, New Mexico.

Anna Nolan Clark, in a 1937 article in *New Mexico Magazine*, detailed how a Syrian peddler brought life to the dying community of Seboyeta in the 1890s and continued to guide the community for the next forty years.[38] His grandson thought it was the kind of town Elias Francis would have liked— somewhat untamed and libertine, with the promise of easy money. He had arrived with the name of Elias Abu Hassan; it is not known when he changed his name, most likely after he returned from Lebanon with his wife and son. Exactly why he chose this family name is not clear; it is possible that he was fond of the French or the family had a French connection; "Francis" was obviously a much better choice in America than "Francois."

Over the years Elias Francis and his son Narciso built a large and multi-faceted family business in western New Mexico. Through their company, Elias Francis and Son, they controlled over 400,000 acres of land, located primarily in the Ignacio Chavez Land Grant. This enabled them to run between thirty and thirty-two thousand sheep and two to three thousand head of cattle. They employed between fifty and sixty men from surrounding communities and customarily hired an additional three to four hundred men during lambing season. The company had an enormous economic impact in the area, which also included the nearby Indian pueblos, Laguna and Paguate. Nasario García, in his *Comadres: Hispanic Women of the Río Puerco Valley*, records the story of Susanita Ramirez de Armijo, who remembered the corn flakes and milk she was introduced to during her youth, because her father earned some money working for "los Árabes" in Seboyeta.[39]

While his son Narciso Francis handled the sheep and cattle business, Elias Francis managed the general store that supplied surrounding communities. (His great-great-grandson still has copies of store ledgers written in Arabic.) In addition he planted an orchard that included peaches, apricots, grapes, and apples.[40] Because of the wetter climate in those years, the family vegetable garden enabled them to sell fresh produce to neighboring communities. Francis's entrepreneurial interests went in many directions. Because Middle Eastern *piñon* nuts were larger than the local variety, he imported several hundred trees from his homeland. Unfortunately, the trees did not acclimate and all died. Elias Francis also experimented with silkworms; they arrived one day at the post office, and his grandson, E. Lee Francis, remembered his grandfather expanding on the intricacies of silk production to his grandchildren and other curious bystanders.

Within a short time after arrival, Elias Francis built a large house in Seboyeta; he raised an American flag in front of the house every morning. Several times a year the Francis's hosted parties; other Syrian families would come to spend several days, feasting, dancing, and playing traditional folk music from the Middle East. Some families came as far away as Trinidad and Walsenburg in southern Colorado. Relatives he had brought over from Mount Lebanon joined in the festivities; they included the Fidel, Hanosh, and Michael families. His nephew, Joseph Hanosh, was a renowned *derbeke* player. Easter was the biggest feast day of the year for the family. There also was a lot of target shooting; Francis was an excellent shot and liked to show off his skills. He never missed the annual trip to Albuquerque during the territorial and later state fairs, where he spent his time skeet shooting and in other similar pastimes.

A number of family anecdotes relate tales of Elias teaching both his son and grandson by what may be called "hands-on-experiences." One of the earliest family stories concerns his son, Narciso, whom he sent out to buy fifty sheep. Someone told Narciso that the best way to tell young sheep from old ones is by the number of teeth they have—younger sheep have fewer teeth. The father was much dismayed when his son returned with a herd of old ewes. His grandson, E. Lee Francis, spent much time with his grandfather, who was especially keen to teach him good business practices. At age fourteen Elias sent E. Lee to Cañoncito with a wagon full of fruit and other merchandise, which E. Lee traded for Navajo rugs that he then sold in Albuquerque for a good profit. On Indian feast days in Laguna, Francis would give his grandson a dollar to start trading and see how much he could earn in a day. On one occasion the young Francis was able to sell an inlaid necklace, bracelet, and ring to a trader for ninety-eight dollars.

E. Lee Francis recalled his grandfather's fascination with snakes; he would catch them with his hands and pull out their fangs with his teeth. Then he would kill them and hang them over a fence like trophies. At other times he tried to hypnotize them by following instructions in a book he had brought from Lebanon. That did not always go well, because he was bitten once. Quickly cutting into his flesh to cut out the venom, he made his grandson swear he would never tell anyone about this mishap. Another time, Francis, who was known for his practical jokes (and a sense of humor that seems strange today), put a defanged snake into a box and brought it to his wife who was sick in bed. One can only imagine her reaction.

Francis was a good drinker by several accounts and sometimes overindulged. On one occasion his wife, Pauline, asked the grandfather of Abe Peña to check on Francis in the attic; he had gone up there the day before and refused to come down. Peña recounted how his grandfather climbed up a ladder to speak with Francis, but quickly retreated after a couple of shots whizzed by him as he stood on the last rung. "I'm not risking my life for this," he remonstrated, "just leave him alone and he'll come down in a day or so, when he is hungry." And so he did.[41]

Francis also considered himself a poet; he regularly submitted his compositions to an Arabic language paper in New York. Subsequent rejections of his work were met with uproar and much swearing: "those Easterners don't know anything about poetry." This interest in poetry was passed on to his great-granddaughter, Paula Gunn Allen, daughter of E. Lee Francis II, who published several volumes of poetry—some celebrating her colorful ancestors. Describing her great-grandfather she wrote in the 1980s:

> There are pictures of my great-
> Grandfather, my father's
> Jide, grandfather—a small,
> Straight man with a moustache.
> He liked to hunt snakes for fun
> Of scaring grandmother, Siti, with.
> Once he got bit and made my father
> Cut the wound with a knife he heated
> Himself in the fire. He sucked the
> Venom and cauterized the gash.
> Grandpa used to hide the whiskey
> Under the stairs so Site
> Couldn't find it. He'd have
> My father fetch it when he wanted
> A drink. He never drank
> before five p.m., and then drank
> most of the night. He gambled
> and kept a woman uptown.
> He used to dress like a prophet
> And peddled rosaries and holy

Pictures in Kansas. They thought
he was insane and spent money
to buy his wares from the Holy Land.
He used to shoot at Siti
When she was carrying water from
The well for supper.⁴²

Elias Francis's family and community both noted his exuberant and quixotic personality. Tapping his teeth with his finger, he would counter anyone questioning his authority with, "¡*Mira! Yo cruce siete mares, y ¿que me dice?*" (Listen, I crossed seven seas and you are telling me?) He quickly forgot the English he had come to America with and spoke Spanish with a generous mingling of Arabic. To his descendants he became a semi-legendary figure, described by his great-granddaughter, Paula Gunn Allen, as a poet, a prophet, farmer, peddler, boozer, magician, owner of a sliver of the "true cross," and much more.⁴³

The people of Seboyeta and the surrounding communities were very fond of the Syrian family that had settled among them. At Christmas time, Don Elias, as he was known among neighbors, distributed oranges that he had ordered from California for everyone in the community. He was godfather to many children and a respected leader in the community. The family participated in Seboyeta social events, as well as in those of surrounding communities and nearby Indian pueblos. Proud of his name and ancestry, Francis commissioned an icon maker in Lebanon to paint a likeness of St. Elias and then had it hung in the Seboyeta church.⁴⁴ Like many other Syrians, the Francis family was devout Catholic and also very patriotic. Ethel Gottlieb Frances remembers the blistering reply of her husband's grandfather when someone asked him what he was. "American, of course," he replied, in a heavily accented voice.⁴⁵ In 1902 the Francis family formally renounced their allegiance to the Turkish sultan and became citizens. Officiating at the event in Los Lunas was Judge Edwin Mechem (senior), father of the future governor, Edwin Mechem.⁴⁶

Don Narciso Francis (1878–1969) was the only child of Elias and Pabla (Pauline Hanosh) Francis. Born in 1878 in Lebanon, but raised in Seboyeta, Narciso grew up speaking Spanish and Arabic. Later the younger Francis learned English, although he had very little formal schooling. Aside from running the family business, Narciso also had an impressive political career—of this more later.

In 1904 Narciso married Filomena Michael, the oldest daughter of Rasheed Michael, who was in business in Albuquerque and had come to New Mexico with his father. They had seven daughters and two sons. E. Lee Francis, the future governor, was the fifth child and first son; his birth was a huge event in the family.

The Depression and extended drought in the 1930s brought an end to the sheep and cattle business of Elias Francis and Son. Elias Francis died in 1931; during the last couple of years of his life he often remarked that his death would change everything. According to E. Lee Francis II, the wild, irreverent, and poetic character of the grandfather differed markedly from that of his conciliatory, more gentle and practical father, Narciso, but the collapse of the business was primarily due to changing economic conditions. When the government bought the Ignacio Chavez Land Grant that they had used for grazing and put a limit of five hundred sheep on the land, the Francis's had to sell both their property and livestock. While they were negotiating with the government, hundreds of sheep died of the drought. They refused to declare bankruptcy, but the people who had worked for them moved away, primarily to Albuquerque, and the community died.

A few months before he died, Elias Francis was planning a trip to Lebanon with his grandson. He always talked about the mountain springs, the apricots, oranges, and grapes from his youth and the village socializing, which he especially missed. E. Lee Francis even considered going to school in Lebanon for a term; obviously, these ideas never materialized.

Reminiscing about the four generations that came before him, E. Lee Francis IV described them as "true Lebanese cowboys"—flamboyant, charismatic, and highly respected in their community. Even his more restrained great-grandfather, Narciso, smoked his customary cigars and played cards with his friends on the day that he died.

It was one o'clock in the morning on October 12, 1909, when the eighteen-year-old Joseph Hanosh arrived in Seboyeta and was met by his aunt, Pauline, wife of Elias Francis.[47] He went to work immediately for his uncle; his wages were fifteen dollars a month. Within a few years he was able to establish his own business, first a store in Bibo and later a trading post at Laguna. The early years were difficult for him and he thought often about going back. "None of us planned to stay," he added wistfully. He missed his family and the old world sociability; moreover, life was much harder than he had anticipated. But he learned Spanish quickly, as well as some Keresan and Navajo, and slowly adjusted to his new life, comfortable both in the Spanish and Indian communities.

In the early years Hanosh had frequent contact with the Native Americans in nearby pueblos. He recalled how impressed he was with their business style, which was based primarily on mutual trust. They did not like sales talk, but were reliable and honest. The Cheramoya family from Laguna became lifelong friends with whom he exchanged bread and home visits. He joined holiday festivities, recalling rooster pulls, Matachines, and St. John's Day celebrations, when he climbed on pueblo roofs to throw presents to those waiting below.

Another special friend was Serafim Marquez, who helped him adjust in the early years. He met very few Anglos; one exception was Julian Kennedy, who had come from Kentucky with Kit Carson and had married a woman from Seboyeta. Whenever necessary, Kennedy would write a letter in English for Hanosh.

Even though he did not go into the livestock business, Hanosh learned how to ride and rope cattle. Aside from his commercial business, he farmed and grew a lot of grapes, Middle Eastern vegetables, and cared for the 150 fruit trees he ordered from Stark Brothers. (One of his Lebanese-style cucumbers grew to fifty-two inches and he had it recorded in *Ripley's Believe It or Not*.)

In 1916 he bought his first car in Albuquerque, a Buick that he drove to Seboyeta, a journey of seven hours that included innumerable railroad crossings and navigating through washed-out parts of the road. It was a good practice for someone who had never driven a car before. A few years later he married Malulia Salamy, whom he had known in Roumieh and who had come with relatives to West Virginia as a sixteen-year-old. Many of their descendants still live in New Mexico. In 1959 he returned to Lebanon for a visit that lasted several months.

Four years after Hanosh arrived in America, he brought over his younger brother Elias. When World War I broke out the following year, Elias enlisted and was sent to Europe. He returned at the end of the war with his citizenship and speaking English. In 1920 another brother, John, and a younger sister arrived in New Mexico.

Joseph Hanosh and family, 1930. Courtesy Kathleen Doherty.

Years after his arrival in New Mexico, Joseph Hanosh's brother, John Hanosh, still recalled the immense distances he had to travel to come to the Southwest. After the train journey from the East Coast, an endless automobile trip on dirt roads took him from Albuquerque to the tiny village of Bibo, where a small building carried a sign: Hanosh Brothers Trading Post. After working several years in Bibo and Seboyeta, John Hanosh and his wife, Rose Fidel, originally from Las Vegas, New Mexico, settled in Mora and started their own business. This would become one of the largest mercantile businesses in northern New Mexico; they also reopened Mora's historic St. Vrain hotel after doing extensive renovations. The hotel was in operation until the 1970s, while the store continued for another decade.[48]

John Hanosh and wife Rose Fidel in their Mora store. Photo by Mark Nohl and Richard Sandoval; Courtesy of *New Mexico Magazine*, February 1982.

Hanosh store in Mora, New Mexico. Photo by Monika Ghattas.

Another Syrian family that settled in Cibola was that of Abdoo Habib Fidel, more commonly known as A. H. Fidel.[49] Coming from the same village of Roumieh, he was related to the other Syrian families in the area. To begin with he peddled groceries, dry goods, and hardware with a horse and wagon to Acomita, McCarthy, Zuni, and to the Navajo Reservation. Shortly thereafter, he opened a general mercantile business on the Laguna Reservation in the village of Vallejos. In recognition of Fidel's commercial contribution to the area, villagers decided to change the name of their community to San Fidel.

San Fidel, New Mexico. Photo by Monika Ghattas.

At the end of World War I, Latife Hanosh Fidel was able to join her husband in New Mexico. Their three young sons had died of malnutrition during the war—an example of the tragedies that befell many families on Mount Lebanon during those years. Three more children were born in the 1920s, before Latife died during childbirth in 1930.

Fidel's business flourished; like other merchants in the area, he had located his store at a point where cars traveled on railroad tracks to cross over arroyos. This careful maneuvering usually attracted an audience and became a popular stopping point. He carried groceries, dry goods, hardware, and anything needed in remote areas. His principal customers were the Indians at Acoma Pueblo, with whom he developed a very good relationship. Over the years he was often consulted about legal issues and other problems the Indians had with government and state agencies. After his wife died, pueblo families took his children home for the weekend or during vacations. For more than seventy years later, his son Joseph, remembered the Chino family at Acoma who often invited him for the holidays during his youth.

After a while some of the pueblo women asked Fidel if they could display their pottery on the porch of his mercantile store. When this merchandise sold quickly, Fidel started to commission the Indians to produce certain wares, like ashtrays, pitchers, and small pots that appealed to the growing tourist trade. Soon orders arrived from many parts of the country, including several museums in the East. Fidel began to focus on the Indian curio business, and with Herbert Harvey, another Syrian merchant from Winslow, Arizona, built wooden boxes to ship the merchandise nationwide. The Fidel Curio Store on Route 66 became a major tourist attraction and was featured on a postcard promoting the highway. In 2009, the former San Fidel store was listed on the National Register of Historic Places for its contribution to the history of the area. Today an art gallery occupies the building.[50]

Joseph Fidel in Grants, New Mexico, 2010. Photo by Monika Ghattas.

Postcard of Fidel's Acoma Indian Curio Store on Highway 66.
Courtesy Pomona Public Library, Pomona, CA.

> Thursday, October 29, 2009
>
> ## UPDATED: San Fidel Shop Becomes National Historic Site
>
> *Associated Press*
>
> SAN FIDEL — A curio shop that sold Native American crafts during Route 66's heyday has been listed on the National Register of Historic Places.
>
> The state Historic Preservation Division says the Acoma Curio Shop in San Fidel was listed on the register because of its association with events that contributed to the broad patterns of history.
>
> Interim State Historic Preservation Officer Jan Biella says the shop is associated with its exclusive trade with Acoma Pueblo. It catered to passing motorists and dealers who specialized in trading Acoma goods along Route 66.
>
> Lebanese immigrant Abdoo H. Fidel built an adobe building in 1916 with a false metal mining front that made the shop a standout.
>
> The curio shop operated from 1937 until 1941.
>
> Today, the building houses an art gallery.

Former Fidel Curio Store declared historic site. *Albuquerque Journal*, October 29, 2009.

One of the three Michael brothers, who came to New Mexico in the late nineteenth century, also settled in the western area of the territory. Merhige Michael (1881–1966) peddled with Naguib Bellamah around Lemitar in the late 1890s; they also had a store in San Macial that was later swept away by one of the periodic floods in the area.[51] Eventually, Michael returned to Mount Lebanon to finish his schooling and marry his childhood sweetheart, Tameme. He returned to New Mexico in 1909; his wife and first son followed in a few months. Seven years later he bought the mercantile business of Abelicio Peña in San Mateo. Abe Peña, the grandson of Abelicio and well-known folklorist of Cibola County, grew up with one of the Michael children and knew the family very well. The Michael household included eleven children and was a prominent part of the community. Spanish and Arabic were spoken at home, and Doña Meme, as Michael's wife was called in the community, was known as a renowned cook and gardener.

In the 1920s Michael began to buy some of the Homestead Act plots that had failed because the 160-acre lots were too small for ranching and did not have enough water. By combining the claims he was able to built an 8,000-acre ranch on which he ran cattle. Like other Syrians in the area, he bought *piñones* from local farmers that were then trucked to Grants for shipment to the East, especially to Brooklyn, where they were sold in Italian grocery stores and by Lebanese street vendors. (The trade in *piñones* was familiar to several Syrian immigrants, because a variety of these nuts was grown both in Mount Lebanon and in the vicinity of Damascus from where they were sent to other areas in the Middle East.) Merchandise for his store was shipped from the Ilfelds in Los Lunas. However, all this came to an end in the Depression. Michael continued to extend credit, even though there was no money in the community; eventually, he was forced to close his business and the family moved to Albuquerque after World War II.

Although somewhat truculent and quick to anger, his neighbors respected Michael for his generosity and participation in community affairs. He loved to play cards, but did not like losing, especially to his wife. Neighbors once saw him angrily trudging down the road out of town. Asked where he was going, he replied that he was going back to Lebanon, "because in the old country women don't try to run everything. Here they want to run everything." On another occasion he tossed his cards into the chamber pot, much to the amusement of his grandson, Toby Michael. There were also boisterous poker sessions in the local pool hall, where tempers sometimes got out of hand. On one occasion a disgruntled ranch hand vowed to shoot every Arab at the card table, except for his *padrino*, Merhige Michael.

Like many other Syrian families, the Michaels subscribed to *Al-Hoda*, the weekly Maronite newspaper published in the East. The family also owned the only radio in town, making Michael not only the source of news from outside the community but also an authoritative interpreter of events—often to the amusement and/or annoyance of some of his neighbors.

Merhige Michael and sons in San Mateo, New Mexico. Courtesy Toby Michael.

Certificate of Citizenship of Michael Michael, oldest son of Merhige Michael. Courtesy Toby Michael.

5

In Search of Economic Opportunities

The hope of making quick money must have attracted several Syrian families to the burgeoning mining and railroad towns in central and northern New Mexico, especially those between Albuquerque and Santa Fe. These towns include Cerrillos, Madrid, Golden, San Pedro, and Waldo, as well as Bland in the foothills of the Jemez Mountains. In the late nineteenth century Cerrillos alone was home to more than three thousand prospectors, attracted there by the possibility of finding gold, silver, and other mineral deposits. They allegedly supported twenty-one saloons, four hotels, and several brothels. This boom did not last very long, but in nearby Madrid coal was mined well into World War II, continuing to stimulate economic activity. Moreover, the railroad that had arrived in the 1880s and connected this area with Albuquerque and northern New Mexico generated considerable momentum.[1]

Therefore, it should not be surprising that a number of Syrian peddlers and later merchants lived and worked in this area. These include Seth Faris and his son-in-law, Joseph Mansour Abu Dagher; the Saad brothers and their cousins, Rasheed and Aziz Michael; possibly Felix Silva, who settled in Bernalillo; and Michael David Koury, who actually worked in the Cerrillos mines. Several others are only remembered by name, because they left no other records.

Among the earliest Syrian peddlers in this area were Rasheed Michael and his brother-in-law Abdo Youssef Saad, who arrived from Roumieh, Mount Lebanon, in 1887 and 1892 respectively. They not only peddled in the Cerrillos area but also in many of the villages between Las Vegas and Socorro. Saad returned home in the late 1890s, but was back in New Mexico a few years later. After World War I

Saad's two sons, Peter A. and Fitty, immigrated to New Mexico and opened a mercantile business in Cerrillos. There they decided to change the spelling of their name, because they did not like the negative connotation of the English pronunciation.[2]

By the mid-1920s economic conditions in Cerrillos were declining and both brothers went on the road, peddling in northern and central New Mexico. (Their families still record the stories of their traveling days through small Hispanic villages, where they were always received kindly and invited to stay for the night. Some of their hosts became lifelong friends, like the family of Don Jose C. Romero in Las Trampas.) In 1930 Peter Sahd moved his family to Taos, where he opened a general store; in later years his adult children extended the business to Ranchos de Taos and Peñasco. Fitty Sahd continued living in Cerrillos, but died there in 1939, leaving his wife, Clara, with five boys under the age of twelve.[3]

Jay and Gabriel Sahd, sons of Fitty and Clara Sahd. Photo by Monika Ghattas.

The Sahd families embraced the culture of northern New Mexico and blended easily with local customs and traditions. They became avid baseball fans and once traveled to Cincinnati to see a special game. Ted Sahd, as the oldest grandson of Peter A. Sahd, spent much time with his popular and colorful grandfather, who strapped him to a pile of pelts in the back of his pickup truck while he peddled in nearby villages. Like several others of his countrymen, Sahd did some bootlegging during Prohibition. One day Judge Carl Hatch, who later became a senator and was a longtime friend and customer, called him about a bootlegger who was in court. He did not want to give the man too hard of a sentence if he was one of Sahd's suppliers. The Sahds also arranged hunting trips for their countrymen a couple of times during the year. After a few days everyone usually came back with a turkey or other wild game; however, the wives were less than pleased when a farmer showed up at one of the Sahd stores asking to be paid for all the turkeys he had recently supplied to the men playing cards at the Costilla cabin. Someone had evidently forgotten to pay him before leaving.

Sahd store in Peñasco, New Mexico. Photo by Monika Ghattas.

Peter and Pattie Sahd with son and grandsons in Peñasco store. Photo by Mark Nohl and Richard Sandoval. Courtesy *New Mexico Magazine*, February 1982.

The Ranchos Trading Post was run by the Sahd family before the great depression and was active through 1981 when George Sahd retired. It was a true community center and the largest general store in the Taos area. The Trading Post consisted of a Soda/Lunch Fountain, Clothing and Drug Store, Canned and Fresh Foods, Butcher Shop, Building Supplies, and Liquor Store. During the depression and WWII trucks went out to deliver goods to the elderly in the community. Every local resident over the age of 25 remembers fondly coming to this active place as a child.

To continue future life for this historic place, we have recreated a portion of the Ranchos Trading Post –"Trading Post Cafe" and strive to once again become a "true community center." We are here to trade "good food" in exchange for "a good time" (and of course a small compensation)!

Join us today and experience a little history with warm friendship and tastefully prepared food!

Welcome!

René and Kimberly

Trading Post Café menu in Taos, New Mexico. Photo by Monika Ghattas.

The Sahds were also active in civic affairs. S. Peter Sahd, who had come to New Mexico as a teenager, headed the Taos Chamber of Commerce and served on the Republican State Central Committee.

There was another Syrian family in Peñasco that had a general store. Coming from Roumieh in 1913 with Fitty Sahd and John Fidel, Asaf Aoun first traveled to Mexico before he arrived in New Mexico. He worked as a peddler for a time and assumed the name of Alex Owen. Eventually he and his wife settled in this northern community where they operated a large mercantile business for many years.

Owen store in Peñasco, New Mexico. Photo by Monika Ghattas.

Rasheed Michael, who arrived in New Mexico in 1887, was the first of three brothers to settle in the state. Fourteen-year-old Azize came in 1894 and a few years later Merhige, who eventually moved to San Mateo. The two older brothers operated the Michael Brothers Mercantile Store in Cerrillos for a few years, but in the late 1890s Azize returned to Mount Lebanon to get married. When he came back in 1903, they decided to open a business in Albuquerque.

The Michael brothers operated several stores over the years, mainly on South Second Street and Third Street and, judging by their advertisements in Worley's city directories, they carried a large variety of goods. The directories also indicate that they employed other Syrian immigrants. (There were four or five Syrian dry goods stores in the city by 1909.[4]) Shortly before World War I, Rasheed sold out to his brother and took his family to Lebanon. It is not clear whether his intent was to return to Lebanon or whether the outbreak of the war forced him to stay there. By the time he returned to New Mexico in 1920, his two older sons were married and brought their own families along.[5]

Both Michael brothers were prominent businessmen and participated in community affairs. They owned bars, grocery stores, and, in later years, a well-known nightclub in the downtown area. They also joined various service organizations, like the Elks and Knights of Columbus. Azize was a member of Alianza Hispanica Americana and served on the city committee that allocated land for the expansion of railroad facilities. Although they were active in local politics, they did not run for office, but worked behind the scenes—organizing voters and promoting their candidates. Rasheed Michael's youngest daughter, Helen Azar, recalled the many local political dignitaries, like Clyde Tingley, Governor Dempsey, and Dennis Chavez, who were regular guests in the family home. Aside from political discussions, there also were frequent card games.[6]

Said (Seth) Faris and Joseph Mansour Abu Dagher also started out as peddlers in the villages of north-central New Mexico and the pueblos along the Rio Grande. At one point they had stores and saloons in Cerrillos, Peña Blanca, Domingo, and in other communities close by. In later years Faris moved to Albuquerque where he opened a grocery store on Fourth Street and invested in land around Bernalillo. He spoke Keres and Spanish, but never mastered English very well or the bureaucratic details of doing business. The family's lifestyle was virtually identical to that of their Hispanic neighbors with whom they socialized and shared traditions.[7]

Born around 1880, Joseph Mansour Abu Dagher left Mount Lebanon as a sixteen-year-old stowaway bound for South America, where he had a brother. But he landed in Cuba instead and went from there to Mexico. After he had worked as a barber and moneychanger for several years, he decided to go north and find a cousin, Moses Abousleman, who was living in Jemez Springs. Traveling by horseback, he arrived in Jemez Springs in 1905, where he opened a barber and butcher shop. A few years later he moved to Algodones and started another business—a pattern that he repeated in Peña Blanca, Cerrillos, and other communities in the area. After his marriage to Seth Faris's oldest daughter, Sallie, in Peña Blanca around 1916, Joseph Budagher (the anglicized name he had adopted) decided to establish a general store in Cochiti Pueblo. But returning from Albuquerque with a wagon full of supplies, the governor of Santo Domingo, Juan Cate, persuaded him to open his store in that pueblo instead.[8]

Although the Budagher family lived in the pueblo only about three years, it was the beginning of a lifelong association with Santo Domingo. They easily integrated into pueblo life and participated in many pueblo functions. Their second son was born there, and Joseph Budagher became an advisor to village elders on issues with the government and often acted as their spokesman; this he continued to do until the end of his life, when some of his sons took over that role. Grateful for his help, the Santo Domingo Indians made him a blood brother and gave him many privileges, such as to hunt and fish on pueblo land—rights that were later passed on to his children.[9]

Joseph and Sallie Budagher with two oldest sons around 1920.
Courtesy Rose Budager Morris.

One of the most memorable events in those years was an uprising in the pueblo on Christmas Day, 1919, when a state mounted police officer, a Colonel Montoya, entered Santo Domingo looking for Indian cattle rustlers. This was illegal, because the pueblo was on federal land and state officials had no jurisdiction there. Rebuked by the Indians, Montoya left, but returned shortly afterward with a posse of twenty to thirty men whom he posted around the pueblo. A skirmish ensued and the Indians arrested Montoya and surrounded the posse. Leo Crane, the area Indian agent, appeased this dangerous confrontation; he had rushed back from Gallup to resolve what he described in his official report to Washington as a "potential massacre" that was narrowly averted.[10]

Budagher's children maintain that it was their father who settled the "last Indian uprising." Although this is not totally accurate judging by Crane's report, Budagher must have had a role in communicating with the Indians. According to his family he was in Albuquerque at the time buying supplies, so the Santo Domingo war chief asked his wife to notify him immediately and tell him to return. When Budagher got off the train in Domingo, several tribal elders were waiting for him and escorted him back to the pueblo, where he counseled them to wait for Crane's arrival. In the end three Indians were arrested and taken to Albuquerque, but Budagher promised the war chief that he would bail them out as soon as possible. Crane commented that the traders in the pueblos often helped the Indians by posting bail and offering other assistance.[11]

Hoping to increase his business, Budagher eventually moved to Domingo, then known as Wallace, where he opened a general merchandise store along the road between Albuquerque and Santa Fe. Also, Domingo had a county school where the older Budagher children were enrolled. Their teacher was Frida Mahboub, the daughter of Syrian immigrants living in Bernalillo.[12]

The fortunes of the family changed dramatically in the early 1930s. First, the store in Domingo burned to the ground. Lost were many personal items, such as Budagher's citizenship papers. They had started rebuilding when they learned that Governor Richard Dillon agreed to reroute the highway several miles to the east, bypassing their location and putting them out of business. As loyal Republicans they were furious with the governor and switched their party affiliation immediately. But voting for Governor Arthur Seligman the following year did not reverse the highway plans, and Budagher was forced to relocate along the new highway. Fortunately, he had learned from a Syrian merchant in Peña Blanca, Gabriel Koury, that there was land available for homesteading, so he took a section and moved his family there. (Gabriel John Nicholas Koury came from Tripoli in northern Lebanon. He may have been the nephew that Nicolas Abdallah in Lemitar brought to New Mexico. Koury later moved to Arizona.) One of the first things that Budagher built was a rock house for his family which served as a school during the day; the county had agreed to send a teacher if he could guarantee enough school-age children. Over the years Budagher operated a variety of businesses at this location: an Indian curio store, a filling station and a small restaurant with a bar that opened the day after Prohibition ended. The Budagher exit still exists on the highway between the two New Mexico cities.[13]

Stone home and school built by Budagher along highway. Photo by Monika Ghattas.

Fiercely independent, daring, and endowed with a good sense of humor, Budagher made a strong impression on his friends and family. He was an avid card player and once won a large tract of land on North Fourth Street in a game with Clyde Tingley. This was years before that area of Albuquerque was developed, and a disappointed Budagher sold the "worthless" marshland for three thousand dollars immediately. Another time he left home to get a midwife for Sallie, in labor with their fourth child. On the way he was sidetracked by a card game and she delivered the baby by herself.[14]

Joseph Budagher in the early 1970s.
Courtesy *Viva El Pasado: A History of the Bernalillo Area* (1973–74).

After his wife died, Budagher and his daughters made a trip back to Lebanon to see relatives and friends. He had never lost contact with them over the years. On the morning of November 15, 1974, he had his customary shot of whiskey and then went deer hunting. Later that day he died. Many Indians from Santo Domingo and Cochiti Pueblo came to his funeral and donated a stained glass window in his honor for the church in Peña Blanca.[15]

The Silva family in Bernalillo is well known in the area for two reasons: the Silva saloon, in operation since 1933, and a gift shop on South Camino del Pueblo that has an outstanding collection of Native American artifacts. Both establishments are owned by descendants of Ferris Shaheen (Hyder), born in 1883 in Biskinta, Mount Lebanon, who came to New Mexico around the turn of the century. Little is known of Shaheen's early years in the area; he probably peddled for a while and may have worked in the Cerrillos mines, an occupation Syrian immigrants did not usually pursue. However, this may explain his early death caused by lung disease. Around 1905 he settled in Bernalillo where he eventually opened a general store and a saloon. He married Dolores Gallegos, from a prominent Algodones family, and their first son George was born in 1910; three more sons and one daughter would follow. It was during these early years in Bernalillo that Shaheen decided to change his name to Silva. One version is that friends and neighbors advised him to do so, because his name did not fit well into the community. So he agreed to use the name of the next person who entered his store—an Indian from Santa Ana with the name of Silva. In another version of the story, Shaheen decided to become Silva, because the Navajos with whom he had frequent contact were amused by his name, which sounded like *bacín*, the Spanish word for chamber pot.[16]

Silva died in 1928; four years later his oldest son, George, was murdered. His body was not found for several months. Many maintain that this was a hate crime related to ethnic tensions in the area; however, it may also have been the tragic consequence of a disputed game of cards. The murderer was identified and the trial received considerable regional publicity. The Hispanic community was very bitter when the accused received a relatively mild sentence and was not reprimanded for the racial slurs he made during the trial. A portrait of George Silva has hung in his nephew's bar in Bernalillo for over seventy years. In 2006, University of New Mexico professor Enrique Lamadrid, with the assistance of David F. García, from the Southwest Hispanic Research Institute and the Chicano/Hispano/Mexicano Studies Program, composed a *corrido* on this tragic event, "El Corrido de George Silva—A Bernalillo Tragedy: Violence, Poetry, and Politics in New Mexico, 1932–33."[17]

Felix Silva on cover of CD: "El Corrido de George Silva: A Bernalillo Tragedy."

This corrido, based on an earlier version composed shortly after the murder, provides an exceptional insight on how the Silva family was perceived in Bernalillo. It makes clear that the they were a respected and integral part of the community, while the evil and bigoted perpetrators of the crime, described as *'serpientes'* (serpents) and *'unos cobardes hueros'* (some gringo cowards) came from outside:

Decían los asesinos, (The murderers said,)
—Eso no es ningún delito (—It is not a crime)
de matar un mexicano (to kill a Mexican)
como cualquier conejito. (Like any little rabbit).

Aquí se acaba el corrido (Here the ballad ends)
Y mucho me alegro yo, (And I am much gratified)
Que hayan sido extranjeros (the murderers were strangers)
Pero nuestra gente no. (and not our own people.)

Several stanzas lament the suffering of the Silva family and describes how the whole community spent days looking for George Silva, a beloved and faithful friend.

James Silva, a younger son, continued operating the family's mercantile store. He was also a trader, especially among Native Americans. Interested in Indian pottery at an early age, he became a major collector and trader of Indian artifacts in the Southwest. Some of his acquisitions are displayed in the curio store owned by his daughters next to the Silva saloon.[18]

There were at least four other Syrian families living in Bernalillo. George and Mary Koury had an antique store for many years, while Lazarro and Nellie Mahboub operated a rooming house and pool hall. Antonio Ziede owned a pharmacy and some members of the Younice family also lived in the community for some years.

Michael David Koury arrived in Cerrillos in 1890 to work in the mines with his uncle. After a few years Koury returned to Mount Lebanon to get married; he then returned to Cerrillos in 1901. (Several brothers and cousins followed and lived in New Mexico and Arizona.) In 1908 the family moved to Santa Fe, because Salome Koury and some of her children could not tolerate the dust of the mines. The family did a lot of peddling; *Sittti* Koury, as Salome was called in later years, contributed by making wine, soap, and beer that she sold on the side. She was a legendary cook in the Syrian community, and the family was the nexus of frequent social gatherings that included Hispanic neighbors and friends. Grandchildren recall reading newspapers to their illiterate grandparents, who entertained them with stories from *One Thousand and One Nights*.[19]

One of the earliest peddlers in the Jemez Mountains was Moses Abousleman. Born in 1869, he arrived in New Mexico in the late 1880s. Abousleman partnered with Nathan Salmon in the early 1890s, but then decided to move south and open a couple of stores in Jemez Pueblo, while he continued to sell dry goods from a horse and wagon in the area. He married a cousin in 1894; Nathan Salmon brought her to New Mexico from the East Coast. The 1900 census shows the couple living with their two daughters in Jemez Pueblo. A few years later both stores burned down and Abousleman decided to move to Jemez Springs; he liked the area and wanted to be closer to the sheep he was pasturing in the Valle Grande and north toward Cuba. With a flock of forty thousand sheep, Abousleman was one of the largest herdsmen in the area.[20]

Moses Abousleman.
Courtesy Tom Abousleman.

The family lived in the pueblo while an Irish contractor began the construction of their home. But before the home was ready, Abousleman was involved in a gun battle with sheep rustlers. The sheriff who accompanied him was fatally shot when they surprised the thieves in their camp; Abousleman received a wound in the arm that left him permanently disabled on one side. While he was convalescing in the pueblo, his wife Edna decided to ride up the canyon and check on their 7,500-square-foot house with its nine bedrooms, which was under construction in Jemez Springs. The builder had remembered to include a Victorian-style parlor with bay windows as requested, plus a central stairwell and indoor plumbing. But he had forgotten about a kitchen. It was added on in the back and the whole episode became a favorite family story.[21]

Abousleman home in Jemez Springs, New Mexico. Photo by Monika Ghattas.

Don Moise, as Abousleman was called in the community, continued with his sheep ranching, but he also opened a mercantile store and saloon in Jemez Springs. (Today the renowned Los Ojos bar and restaurant are located on this property.) In addition, he traded in wool and pelts and invested in real estate. The well-to-do family enjoyed a comfortable lifestyle, which surviving photographs record. Periodic trips to Albuquerque took two days with horse and wagon; the first night was spent in Zia Pueblo and the next in Bernalillo, before they boarded the train to Albuquerque. Their eight children were sent to boarding schools in Albuquerque and Santa Fe; all five daughters were college educated and three of them had advanced degrees. They were very active in the community for many years; Josephine Abousleman Shepherd was instrumental in getting Jemez Springs incorporated and was elected mayor several times. Her sister, Lilian Abousleman Sotel, was superintendent of schools, and, with Barbara Abousleman, taught in the school system for many years.[22]

Tom Abousleman in 2008, Jemez Springs, New Mexico. Photo by Monika Ghattas.

Moses Abousleman in Jemez Canyon. Courtesy Marian Sotel.

Abousleman daughters. Courtesy Marian Sotel.

Abousleman often remarked on how the Jemez Mountains and the sheep reminded him of home. He planted a large garden and orchard in the canyon, and their home became a favorite destination for Syrian families living in Albuquerque and Santa Fe. It was a multilingual household, where Arabic was spoken at home and Spanish in the community. In addition, Abousleman taught himself how to read and write in English. He offered land to the Franciscan sisters to build a convent and church in Jemez Springs, but they chose the pueblo instead. As devout Catholics, the family set aside a special room for traveling priests who stopped by periodically.[23]

Like his cousin, Joseph Budagher, Abousleman maintained excellent relations with the Indians of Jemez Pueblo. He had a great deal of respect for Indian customs and was often consulted about important issues in the pueblo. His son, Tom, remembered an incident from his youth, when he and his brother found some prayer sticks in caves close to Soda Dam. Their father ordered them to return them immediately to where they had found them.[24]

Shortly after the turn of the century, Edna Abousleman's two brothers came from Lebanon and lived with them for some time. One of the brothers went back after a few years, but George Abousleman stayed and served in World War I. Upon his return from the war he married Margarita Maestas, the daughter of his business partner. They eventually settled in Bernalillo, where they bought a house large enough for boarding lodgers. The family also opened a general store, a saloon, and several other businesses in later years.[25]

Sarah, Uncle Joe, Moses, Uncle George, Edna, Theresa (cousin) Rose, Barbara, Josephine, & Fred (Lillian, Marcel & Tom not shown)

Abousleman family. Courtesy Marian Sotel.

Moses Abousleman died in 1934, and his wife died a few months later. By that time the Depression had impacted the family; they had extended more than $30,000 in credit which they were unable to collect. Daughter Lilian Abousleman Sotel bought a portable saw to cut lumber for the railroad, and this became a major source of support for the family until the outbreak of World War II.[26]

Also listed as living in Jemez in the 1900 census were Ragais and Rufina Unes, who were Abousleman's longtime partners. They were probably related to other families, more commonly known as Younice or Younis who settled in Dixon, Cuba, Taos, Bernalillo, and other New Mexico communities and were originally from Roumieh. Tobias and Gabriel Younis are notated as peddlers in the 1900 Bernalillo census. In an article in *La Herencia* about the Lebanese in New Mexico, Arnold Vigil included a photograph of Tobias Younis with his family of five children.[27]

~~~

At an age when most men have been retired for years, Abdullah Samuel Adelo works as a certified court interpreter for the State of New Mexico. In his late eighties, he is fluent in Spanish and English and gets along with "survival" Arabic. He is a regular contributor to *La Herencia*, a publication dedicated to the preservation of Hispanic culture and history, and he was the longtime author of a bilingual column, "Vistas Hispañas," in the *Santa Fe New Mexican*. Several years ago he was named one of Santa Fe's living treasures, and he is listed among prominent Hispanic individuals in the community. As a lawyer working for Gulf Oil, he worked and traveled extensively in earlier years, including in the homeland of his father and grandfather. He is not only an excellent source of information for his own family but also for many other Syrian families in this state whom he has known during his long lifetime.[28]

A. Samuel Adelo in 2009. Photo by Monika Ghattas.

His father, Assad Abdullah Abu Habib, from Roumieh, changed his name to Samuel Adelo when he arrived in this country a few years before the outbreak of World War I. Like most of his countrymen, Adelo started as a peddler in northern New Mexico. Equipped with a horse and wagon that the Ilfelds in Las Vegas gave him on credit, he sold and bartered in pots and pans, wool, pelts, and household items in the Puerto de Luna area and in small villages and ranches around Las Vegas. Sometimes he was on the road for over two months, until he had to return for new stock. In 1917 he decided to enlist and, rewarded with his citizenship, he returned to New Mexico, where he married Lourdes Varela Silva. The couple settled in Pecos, where they opened a general store in the early 1920s.[29]

Adelo store in Pecos, New Mexico. Photo by Monika Ghattas.

Similar to what happened in other Syrian families, Adelo's father had peddled in the area in the late 1880s and 1890s; he opened a store in Roy, but returned to Mount Lebanon. Likewise, Adelo had two brothers in northern New Mexico, who dealt in cattle and *piñones*; one of them had a business in Santa Fe for a few years, but both returned home eventually.[30]

In an article published in the *Santa Fe New Mexican* on November 10, 1977, on the occasion of his eighty-fifth birthday, Adelo was described as "Lebanese, but all New Mexican." This was perhaps a very appropriate description of a man who loved New Mexico but who also maintained ties to his homeland and instructed his children to be proud of their heritage. His son described the family home as a rich mixture of two cultures, where children were exposed to multiple languages, a variety of food, Arabic and Spanish music, and frequent social gatherings.[31]

The Adelo store in Pecos prospered, especially when the American Metals Company started mining for lead and zinc in Terrero. In addition, there was much lumbering in nearby mountains to meet the demand for railroad ties and mine stoking. Servicing a wide area, the business always included a lot of bartering that involved much socializing on the side; it was not unusual for customers to enter the store with a five-hundred-pound sack of *piñones* to exchange for food staples or animal feed. And visitors to the Pecos region always stopped by the store, because it was the community information center and had the only telephone in the area. A. Sam Adelo recalled the frequent trips he took to Santa Fe with his father. They spent hours at wholesalers, visiting and buying merchandise. Before heading home, they had to call on every Syrian family in town; otherwise, there would be problems.[32]

During the summer months, the Adelos organized frequent picnics in the nearby mountains for the Syrian community. These festivities always included a lot of food, a couple of barbecued lambs, and Middle Eastern music improvised by Fitty Sahd on the derbeke.

Adelo was very active in the community of Pecos, especially in matters that concerned education. He had taught school in Mount Lebanon and had come to this country intent on continuing his studies. In his new home he served on the school board and brought the Sisters of Divine Providence to Pecos to teach in the local high school his children attended. (Religious orders were permitted to teach in New Mexico public schools until 1951.[33]) His oldest son, A. Samuel Adelo, later enrolled in St. Michael's boarding school in Santa Fe and then continued his education at the University of Notre Dame.[34]

In addition, Adelo was involved in state politics. In the 1930s, he served as state senator from San Miguel County. His son remembered helping his father with this campaign; it was almost entirely in Spanish.[35]

But Adelo also retained a certain affinity for his homeland. He spoke often about his youth and kept in touch with events in Lebanon. He admonished his children to honor their background and not discriminate against anyone. In Pecos he hired a stonemason to built a house, similar in style to those he remembered from his youth. With Nathan Salmon in Santa Fe, he organized the Syrian-Lebanese Club that met at the Lensic Theater during the 1930s and 1940s. After he retired in 1952, Adelo began his visits to Lebanon, often staying for years at a time.

Samuel Adelo on his 85th birthday in Pecos, New Mexico. *The Santa Fe New Mexican*, November 10, 1977.

There is little information about Joseph Fidel, who had a business on Bridge Street in Las Vegas and who must have been one of the earliest Syrian immigrants in the state. Yet Fidel was evidently a pivotal person in the Roumieh community; he welcomed friends and relatives from his hometown when they arrived. It was Uncle Joseph, in Las Vegas, who became the first contact in New Mexico for his four nephews with the same surname, as well as for the Sahd and Adelo families, the Michael brothers, Fuad Amin, and Fidel Merhige. One of Joseph Fidel's daughters married John Hanosh, and together they operated a grocery store and hotel in Mora for many years. Reminiscing about her father's early peddling, Rose Fidel Hanosh talked about the bandits that used to harass him on the road.[36]

Born in 1884, Fidel Merhige lived with his uncle, Joseph Fidel, in Las Vegas while he peddled with horse and wagon in the pre-World War I era. Just before the outbreak of the war, he returned to Roumieh to get married and then came back in 1919 with his wife and the youngest of their three daughters. Six months later the couple opened a store in San Juan Pueblo, where they lived for the next twelve years. Thus the Merhige children grew up speaking Tewa, Spanish, and Arabic at home. The family's next investment was a farm and a large apple orchard, similar to the ones the family had owned in Mount Lebanon.[37]

The family moved to Española after Merhige bought a clothing store; he later opened a general store, several movie theaters, and the Zia nightclub there. At the same time he invested in an 8,000-acre ranch in Tierra Amarilla, where he ran part of his sheep. (New Mexico historian, Robert Tórrez, remembered his father mentioning the land of "los Árabes" close to their property in Tierra Amarilla.) The rest of his sheep were at the Baca Ranch and at Black Mesa. During the summer months, Fidel Merhige, with his brother Mike, traveled to the mining camps of southern Colorado and Arizona selling chiles and *piñones*. This was good business, because they earned some hard currency; at home most everything was on credit.[38]

Merhige Lane in Española, New Mexico. Photo by Monika Ghattas.

The Merhige family adjusted very well in northern New Mexico. Their son, John, born a year after they arrived, remembered his parents' frequent discussions about the Indian and Hispanic customs and beliefs they found similar to those in their homeland, such as the emphasis on family honor, the role of storytelling in socializing children, and the importance of religious rituals.

~~~

There were other Syrian families who settled in northern New Mexico. However, they did not come from Mount Lebanon, but rather from Zahle, a medium-size market and railroad town located in the Bekaa valley on the other side of Mount Lebanon; it was also a major trading center between Beirut and Damascus. Many of these families came through Denver and had relatives in southern Colorado, especially in the mining communities around Walsenburg, Trinidad, and in the San Luis Valley. They generally did not invest in livestock or in ranching, but were primarily traders and merchants. Most of them were Melkite Catholic; in fact, the Syrian community in Trinidad was large enough to built a Melkite Church in 1914, which was active until the 1960s.[39]

Belonging to this group from Zahle was the large Macaron family that had general stores in Springer, Farley, Wagon Mound, Maxwell, and Raton. Although the Springer store was sold recently, the family celebrated its eighty-fifth year in business in 2005. The Springer public library is named after Fred Macaron, the son of Joseph and Lillie Macaron, who bought the city market when they arrived in 1920. Another branch of the family in Raton also operated a general merchandise store and later diversified into other fields. The George Macaron Family Charitable Foundation endows a variety of Raton community projects.[40]

Lillie Macaron was the daughter of Sleman David Nsayer (later known as Sleman David) and Elmas Sawaya, who ran several stores in northern New Mexico. David had joined a Turkish acrobatic team shortly after he arrived in America and spent some time with Buffalo Bill's Wild West Show and the Barnum and Bailey Circus. This led him to southern Colorado and finally to Cimarron where he opened his first store in 1914. He became a prominent member of the community and participated in its efforts to bring the Boy Scout program to the area. The family eventually moved to Springer where they set up another store and lived in the old Reform School that now houses the Santa Fe Trail Museum.⁴¹

Macaron store in Springer, New Mexico, 1918. Courtesy Springer Public Library.

Springer Public Library. Photo by Monika Ghattas.

Also operating a business in the same area was the Skaff family that was related to the Macarons. They had a packinghouse where Sam Adelo came with his father to buy chile for the store in Pecos. In Colfax and Union County were several Syrian merchants who had come from Zahle. They include Habeb Azar, Joseph Kouri, Albert Abraham Kouri, and Toufic Smith in Des Moines, who had translated his Arabic name, Haddad, into the appropriate English equivalent. The Azar family had relatives in Raton and in southern Colorado. Charles Bonahoom was a bricklayer in Raton who became an amateur archaeologist when he participated in the 1926 excavations in Folsom, New Mexico, where findings led to a major revision in the field.[42] He may have known another Syrian immigrant, Elias Cory, who married Dovie Posey in Folsoms' St. Joseph's Church in 1912 and later bought the 'haunted' Urraca Mesa, now located on the Philmont Scout Ranch.[43] The Maloof and Fram families in Las Vegas were also related to Syrian immigrants with the same or similar names in southern Colorado; all had come originally from Zahle. Also belonging to this group were the Keloffs; they settled in the Farmington area, where they still have a variety of business interests.[44]

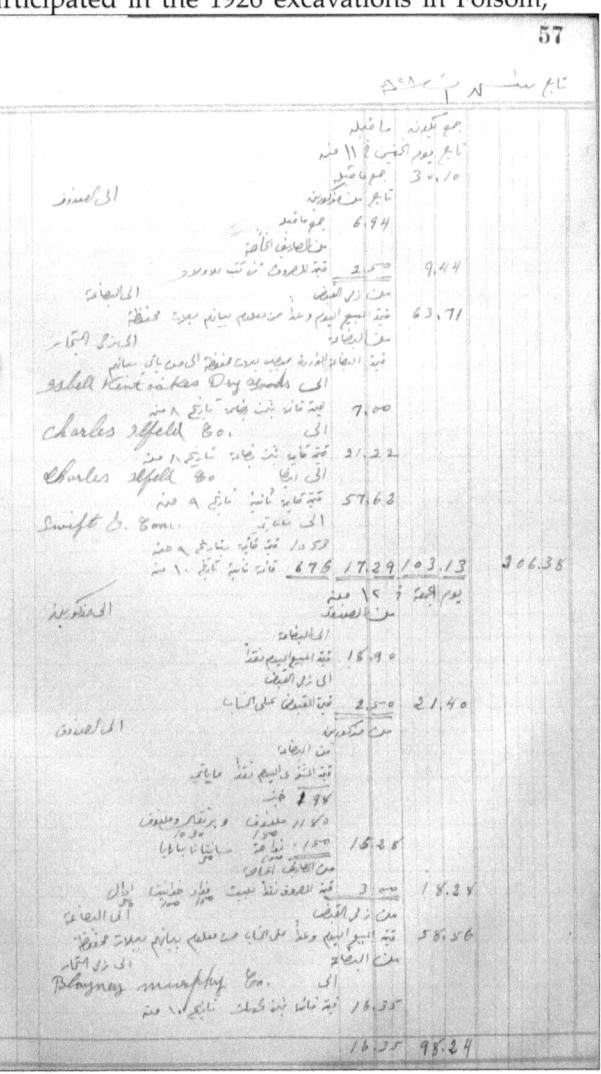

Azar's Raton grocery store ledger. Raton Store Ledger, 1907–38 (MSS 297 BC, box 13), Center of Southwest Research, University Libraries, University of New Mexico.

In conclusion, it is clear that a considerable number of Syrian immigrants first peddled and then settled in scattered communities of central and northern New Mexico. Although some of these were traditional Hispanic villages and Indian pueblos, a considerable number were relatively new towns that appeared in the last part of the nineteenth century-the consequence of railroad expansion and new mining camps. By setting up general stores, the Syrians provided necessary merchandise and services, filling a niche created by rapidly changing circumstances. At the same time, their cross-cultural diplomatic skills and linguistic talents helped them forge and sustain long-lasting relationships with Native Americans that were based on good will and mutual respect.

6

Assimilation: Soy Mexicano casi[1]

The assimilation of minorities into mainstream American life has become the subject of some vigorous discussions in recent years. Not only is it difficult to determine the point at which a population group can be described as assimilated, but also the very definition of assimilation is problematic. In addition, it is challenging to formulate a solid description of what constitutes "typical" American life, given the great diversity of people and cultures in this country.

Some historians engaged with immigration history distinguish between assimilation and acculturation. The latter term supposedly suggests that immigrants pursue a different posture in public life, where they try to accommodate to American ways as much as possible, while they retain ethnic customs in their private lives. This distinction would be difficult to follow in New Mexico, where Syrians socialized with Hispanic neighbors quickly and easily. The only obvious difference between home and public life was that they may have spoken Arabic at home and prepared some ethnic food. But these particulars alone cannot be seen as a conscientious effort to maintain a distinct lifestyle. (There are numerous examples of third- and fourth-generation descendents, who have opened New Mexican restaurants with their Hispanic spouses, but continue to prepare Arabic food at home, especially for notable occasions.)

The process of acculturation often includes painful choices of values, especially when it involves the next generation. What beliefs, customs, and values should be taught and encouraged in children? How important is the preservation of the native language? There were heated discussions about these issues in the Arabic press, where the absence of historical and cultural roots in Middle Eastern immigrants did not go unnoticed, and many publications included long discourses on the advisability of maintaining some cultural and linguistic connections to the home country and instilling them in the next generation. Those who supported a rapid adoption of American ways were labeled "Americanists," while "nativists" insisted that there should be a serious effort to preserve the old traditions. The passage of time eventually solved these issues in favor of the first group. These questions never received any serious consideration in New Mexico, where the small number of immigrants and their rapid assimilation muted these issues.[2]

There are various ways of measuring the degree of assimilation an immigrant population has achieved. These include fluency in the dominant language, participation in community affairs, and the adoption and integration of cultural norms and values that are a part of the new environment. These tools for evaluating the integration of the Syrian immigrants into New Mexico communities are readily available and indicate that the process of assimilation differed in many respects from what was taking place elsewhere. Most importantly, the strong similarity in lifestyle and culture between Hispanic New Mexico and the Syrians from Mount Lebanon resulted in complaisant accommodation.

Before detailing the specific features and characteristics of Middle Eastern immigrants that facilitated their integration into the southwestern environment, it is noteworthy to mention an article published in the *Journal of American Folklore*, "Notes on the Language and Folk-Usage of the Rio Grande Valley (With Special Regard to Survivals of Arabic Custom)."[3] Published in the late 1890s, this article was written by Captain John G. Bourke, who was stationed at Fort Craig in 1870—almost twenty years before the first Syrians arrived in the Southwest. Bourke must have been thinking about the Moorish influences still noticeable in the Hispanic culture of this area; studying his observations, one feels that he is listing the specific conditions and features of life in New Mexico that would expedite the acculturation of the immigrants who were to come twenty years later. Comparing Hispanic and Arab culture, he notes a large variety of similarities that range from architectural styles and food preferences to filigree jewelry and church customs. He delves into many minute details of everyday life that are rooted in Arabic culture, such as burial and birthing customs, treatment of the sick, the role of proverbs and fables, and the significance of the "evil eye."

> THE JOURNAL OF
> # AMERICAN FOLK-LORE.
> Vol. IX. — APRIL–JUNE, 1896. — No. XXXIII.
>
> NOTES ON THE LANGUAGE AND FOLK-USAGE OF
> THE RIO GRANDE VALLEY.[1]
>
> (WITH ESPECIAL REGARD TO SURVIVALS OF ARABIC CUSTOM.)
>
> SYNOPSIS OF CONTENTS.
>
> Introductory.
> Dress of Mexicans.
> Jewelry.
> Houses, Architecture, etc.
> Furniture.
> Meals.
>
> Gambling.
> Correr el Gallo.
> *Bailes* and *Tertulias*.
> Christenings.
> Courtship and Marriage.
> Mortuary Ceremonies.

John G. Bourke's article listed on the title page of *The Journal of American Folk-Lore.*

Recent studies of both Hispanic New Mexico and nineteenth-century Mount Lebanon confirm Bourke's observations both about the function and the characteristics of these practices. Marta Weigle, in *The Lore of New Mexico*, describes the importance of rites of passage in Hispanic New Mexico, such as marriages, baptisms, and funerals, while Samir Khalaf in his investigation of nineteenth-century village life on Mount Lebanon highlights the significance of the same rituals.[4]

These diverse similarities eased the integration of Middle Eastern immigrants into the Hispanic culture of New Mexico. Examples that mirror analogous practices can be gleaned from immigrant narratives. For example, the mother and grandmother of the young E. Lee Francis made a pilgrimage, partially on their knees, to a local shrine to pray for his recovery after he swallowed a screw. They also vowed to dress him in a miniature monastic cloak for several years if he survived. In the village of Seboyeta this event was not considered unusual. Religious pilgrimages continue to be an important part of New Mexico culture, and Francis felt that his blue cloak and cord were not out of place in the community. Viewed from the opposite perspective, the Syrians were not surprised to witness the Hispanic practice of hiring *plañideras*, professional mourners, who lent an appropriately somber setting to funerals. Similar practices were observed on Mount Lebanon.[5]

When examining the specific steps in Syrian immigrants' acculturation process, it is important to consider their cultural values and background and how these expedited or delayed their entry into American life. Similar to some other immigrants, especially those from southeastern Europe and the Mediterranean area, the people from Mount Lebanon had no strong political or historical roots. Several historians have referred to them as a people "truly without a country," where patriotism was defined as a form of loyalty to church and family.[6] According to David Lowenthal, professor of geography and heritage studies, this was not a unique situation. He found that the lack of patriotism and basic understanding of history and geography were evident in all immigrant groups, even in a country as westernized as France, where many peasants rarely ventured farther than a few miles from their native villages.[7] However, the Syrians were unusually detached from their homeland. They did not identify with the central government in Istanbul, had little if any contact with its representatives, and were by and large apolitical. Neither nationalism nor patriotism had made an impact in their native lands; instead, they were more affected by the turbulent conditions and periodic oppressions that marked the end of the Ottoman empire.

In the eastern and central areas of the United States, Syrians were confronted with a society that was very patriotic and keenly aware of its unique historical unfolding. Settling into their own communities for mutual support, they could not intermingle with their Anglo neighbors until they were familiar with the American way of life and understood and adopted prevailing values and mores.

Circumstances of life were very different in New Mexico. The predominant Hispanic population, similar to the experiences of the Syrian immigrants, was estranged from the central government in Washington. The consequences of the Mexican American War in the late 1840s had made little impact on their daily lives, and few identified with their new political superiors in the nation's capital. Historians have described the people as apathetic and disinterested in the distant government. Similar to Syrian experiences, the Hispanic population did not see New Mexico as a political community. In addition, their lifestyle, their culture, and even their language continued to differ significantly from other areas of the country. Thus the Syrians with their equally apolitical orientation and generally weak historical roots were able to integrate into New Mexico society with relative ease.[8]

Among other parallels between the two groups was religion, possibly the most critical form of identity in both cultures; in fact, the institutional church assumed many characteristics of a nation-state. With the exception of one prominent Muslim family, all of the Syrians who came to New Mexico were Catholics. More specifically, the majority was Maronite, the dominant Christian rite in Mount Lebanon that dates from the early Christian period in the Middle East. The rest of the newcomers were either Melkite (Greek Catholic) or Greek Orthodox. All three groups were compatible with the Roman Catholicism of New Mexico's Hispanic population. Thus they immediately encountered a familiar and significant institution that helped them integrate into the native community.[9]

In the East many Catholic immigrants, including those from the Middle East, encountered considerable hostility because of their religion. Many Americans were afraid that the newcomers would alter the predominantly Protestant orientation of the country, and they perceived various subversive tendencies in the Roman Church. New Mexico's attempt to attain statehood in the late nineteenth century was frustrated for years in large part because of the preponderance of the Catholic Church, interpreted as an indisputable sign of the ignorance, superstition, and backwardness of its inhabitants. Also, as more and more migrants arrived in the New World, it was obvious that there were considerable differences between the various ethnic Catholic churches. For the Irish, the church was a symbol of nationalism and unity against the hated English dominance; the Italians, on the other hand, were often stridently anticlerical and saw the church as a suppressive institution. Ethnic differences between population groups were sometimes acted out in religious terms. The Irish, for example, were highly suspicious of the Syrians' churches, especially as they began to move into Irish neighborhoods and workplaces.[10]

None of these religious issues arose in New Mexico; instead, the newcomers were immediately drawn into the existing religious community. They assumed the religious obligations of their new parishes and added the saints and feast days of Hispanic New Mexico to their religious calendar. Several families, like the Abouslemans, Tabets, Francises, and Budaghers mentioned their pride in being chosen community *padrinos* in charge of the local church saint and assuming other religious duties. As godparents to the children of new neighbors and friends, they blended almost seamlessly into the community. Both Elias Francis and Merhige Michael in San Mateo participated in the semisecret Penitente Brotherhood, while others joined the Knights of Columbus and various Catholic service organizations.[11]

Next in importance to their faith was the centrality of family. Kinship ties were honored and nurtured and functioned as an important form of community identification. All members of a family were obliged to support one another, both economically and psychologically, while children were expected to honor their elders. Peer pressure ensured conformity and family cohesion. The immigrants' social precepts and emphasis on family values were virtually the same in the conservative Hispanic villages of New Mexico. Likewise, both cultures valued hospitality to strangers and the importance of village sociality.[12]

Like their Hispanic neighbors, the Syrians had a strong parochial predilection that superseded a national identity. The village was the center of their life and, aside from religion and family, defined their sense of place. In this form of identity, family names were often linked with specific villages. This was also the custom in territorial New Mexico, where people did not identify themselves with a region, but with belonging to a village.[13] Traditional Hispanic village life with its complex social system of village elders, patriarchy, and respect for conventional mores was similar to that of Mount Lebanon. Likewise, arranged marriages with their meddling matchmakers were part of both cultures. Also familiar was the role of community *patrón*, sharecropping, and various cooperative enterprises that defined daily life, such as communal harvesting, preparation of food, and the seasonal maintenance of irrigation systems.

Other details of village life mirrored each other, especially in matters regarding folk medicine, *curanderas*, medicinal herbs, the interpretation of omens, and other healing practices. Eliseo "Cheo" Torres, writing on Mexican folk healing in *Curandero: A Life in Mexican Folk Healing*, comments on the close link of southwestern medicinal practices to Arabic traditions. Similar information comes from Meldrum Wylder in his *Rio Grande Medicine Man*, who writes that both Native Americans and the Hispanic population commonly used Moorish healing herbs. Descendants of the early immigrants recall their parents' familiarity with local *curanderos* and medicinal herbs; evidently, they were often consulted about remedies and other health-related questions.

Women, like Sitti Koury in Santa Fe and Meme Abousleman in Jemez Springs, advised on difficult births, while others assisted local midwives.[14]

> Mr. and Mrs. Moses Abousleman
>
> invitan a usted y apreciable familia para que los honren
>
> con su presencia al enlace de sus hijas
>
> Sarah Adema y Fred Emanuel Nassour
>
> y
>
> Lillian Marie y Dr. Constantine A. Sotel,
>
> el Martes en la manana dia catorce de Junio
>
> de mil nuebecientos beintiuno a las
>
> diez y media en la iglesia de
>
> Nuestra Senora del Rosario en

Abousleman wedding invitation in Spanish. Courtesy Marian Sotel.

Both cultures shared a strong belief in "the evil eye" and devised ways of alleviating its effect. Torres describes how the afflicted could be helped by massaging the body with a raw egg. Aside from pinning good luck charms on children's clothing, Syrians also relied on eggs to cure difficult problems, like headaches and muscle pains. Rasmieh Hindi's nephew remembered his aunt breaking an egg on a child's forehead to reduce a fever.[15]

(The similarities of Hispanic and Syrian culture are evident in Moussa's Castle, a folk art museum in the mountains south of Beirut that describes and illustrates the handicrafts of traditional Lebanese villages. Included in the displays are examples of textiles and their production: wool shearing, weaving, and dying; working clay and shaping pottery; plus bread making on a round stone surface heated by wood underneath. Only in the depiction of brewing and serving pungent Arabic coffee does this scene differ from what could be portrayed in a similar museum in the Southwest.)

It was not only the village setting that attracted the newcomers but also the surrounding landscape of mountains and forests. In fact, it is curious that many Syrians coming from Roumieh remarked about the similarity of the landscape: the mountains, the fresh air, the pine forests, and the generally rural and pastoral quality in this area. It is interesting that Fray Angélico Chávez, in *My Penitente Land* dwells on the "pervasive pastoral and spiritual themes in traditional Spanish life that are shared by the people of Palestine, Castile, and Hispanic New Mexico.[16] Sam Adelo, John Amin, and others recalled how their fathers commented not only on the similarities in landscape, but that they also thought the people looked like their neighbors at home. How different these impressions and experiences were from those of their countrymen who settled in the urban and industrialized areas of the East and Midwest.

Assimilation was also expedited by other, often unexpected, circumstances: the Spanish language contained an abundance of Arabic words; everyday life in Hispanic New Mexico included expressions and references that were virtually the same in Arabic, like *alcalde, zaguán, alforja, acequia, jarra, alberca,* the colonial measurements of *fanega* and *arroba, alquilar* and *ahorrar,* plus many more, including ¡ojalá!, a derivative of *insha'Allah*—God willing in Arabic. Many words for clothing are the same, as well as those for herbs, spices, food, and fruit, as, for example, *arroz, azúcar, aceite, aceituna, zumaque* and *albaricoque.* It is not surprising that almost all of the immigrants became fluent in Spanish, often forgetting the little English they had learned at home or on the way.[17]

In one of his most recent books, *Arab/American: Landscape, Culture, and Cuisines in Two Great Deserts,* American ethnobiologist Gary Nabhan mentions the many plant and place names that came from the Arabic and Berber into Spanish. Included are terms used by Southwest cowboys and ranchers, like *azote, jinete,* and *argollas,* as well as descriptive references for sheep, horses, and cattle.[18]

Even the customary diet of Hispanic New Mexico had a strong resemblance to Mount Lebanon, where lamb and mutton were commonly consumed with a variety of legumes. The Syrians used sumac berries and wild thyme in their dishes—their New World equivalents all readily found in this area. Tibo Chavez, in *Folklore of the Rio Abajo,* lists the many herbs in use that originated in the Middle East, like anise, cilantro, *albahaca* (basil), *asafrán* (saffron), and others. One of the New Mexico Federal Writers' Project reports of the Depression era includes a dish of "cabrito with hulled wheat seasoned with coriander, onion and garlic" that reads like a Middle Eastern recipe, while Nabhan mentions a Persian-Arabian dish with lamb and garbanzos in Cleofas Jaramillo's 1939 cookbook, *The Genuine New Mexico Tasty Recipes*. But perhaps most surprising of all were the *piñones*. Where else in the United States would they have come across these nuts that are essential in many Middle Eastern dishes? In fact, *piñones* became a big export item for local Syrians, like Sam Adelo, Merhige Michael, and Elias Francis, who annually shipped hundreds of sacks to Syrian and Italian wholesalers in the East.[19]

Quick assimilation was also the pattern for those Syrians who settled in railroad and mining communities, as well as those who came to Albuquerque, Santa Fe, Las Vegas, and Bernalillo. Since they were few in number, they did not congregate in specific areas, but opened their businesses in the downtown district, often living close to their stores. Economic and practical reasons forced them to intermingle quickly with their neighbors. In Albuquerque many resided in the same vicinity as the Italian immigrants; descendants of several families speak about the close relations between the two ethnic groups who frequently worked and socialized together.[20]

Not only did the newcomers find a familiar environment in New Mexico, they also were able to pursue similar livelihoods. Given the complicated land tenure system in Mount Lebanon and the general scarcity of arable land, many of the immigrants had engaged in some commercial and entrepreneurial activities to supplement their income. They followed this practice in New Mexico, where they opened general stores with money saved from peddling and then continued to sell on the road part time or invest in livestock and ranching. Others expanded into real estate and entered the entertainment business. Self-employment was their ideal, and many were able to achieve this goal.

Intermarriage is an irrefutable indication of assimilation that seldom occurs in the first immigrant generation. But New Mexico was an exception. Although many Syrians in the first generation returned home to get married or bring back a wife, a significant number married local Hispanic women. These include George Abousleman, brother-in-law of Moses Abousleman in Jemez Springs; one of the Salome brothers in Belen; Alex Hindi in Duran; Sam Adelo from Pecos; Nicolas Abdallah, who married the daughter of a Lemitar merchant; and brothers Gabriel and Tobias Younice. Mixed marriages were, of course, even more frequent with the second generation, even though some parents made a concerted effort to encourage their children to choose a mate from one of the other Lebanese families. (Merhige and Meme Michael refused to attend the marriage of their oldest son, because he insisted on marrying the daughter of one of their Hispanic neighbors. Fortunately, their displeasure was short-lived and they became very fond of her.) The possibility of marriages between Syrians and outsiders was not even considered in the Arabic press, where this controversial topic only centered on the increasing frequency of marriages between Syrians of different Christian sects, such as a Maronite groom and a Greek Orthodox bride.

An early participation in community affairs and in politics illustrates the successful assimilation of Syrian immigrants in New Mexico. Very few first generation Americans, especially those from Eastern Europe, the Mediterranean area, or from places other than northern Europe, entered the public sphere. Often undereducated, unfamiliar with American life, and primarily focused on making a living, they remained outside of the issues that affected their American contemporaries. In New Mexico, however, several first-generation Syrians took an active role in public affairs. Sam Adelo, for example, served as mayor of Pecos and later as state senator from San Miguel County. George Goze in Magdalena served on the Socorro County Commission, as did Narciso Francis in Cibola County. Raymond Shaya ran twice for mayor of Santa Fe, albeit unsuccessfully. Naguib Bellamah became postmaster in Veguita, shortly after he arrived there in 1913. Many of the Syrian immigrants were interested in education issues and served on school boards and in similar community positions.[21]

Narciso Francis, born in Roumieh in 1878 and in New Mexico by the early 1890s, was the most prominent public figure among early Syrian immigrants. As a protégé of Solomon Luna, he was selected as jury foreman in a Silver City trial in 1904 and then served as a justice of the peace. He helped establish the Valencia County school system and became a member of its first Board of Education. But his most important accomplishment was his election to the Second and Third New Mexico Legislatures in 1914 and 1916 respectively. (He would return to the legislature in Santa Fe several more times in later years.) One of his achievements there was the passage of the bimonthly wage act. He was probably the first Syrian in the United States elected to a political office, especially to one so prestigious.[22]

E.Lee Francis. Courtesy E. Lee Francis IV.

Narciso Francis. Courtesy E. Lee Francis IV.

Francis, a fairly recent immigrant, joined the Liberty Immigration Society in 1910, a national organization, not related to the New Mexico Board of Immigration that disbanded in 1912. His son, E. Lee Francis, was especially proud of this, because he had his father's certificate hanging in his living room. The preamble of the society stated that it was organized: "For the purpose of agitating for a liberal legislation of immigration in these United States and to devise a system of education preparing the immigrants for intelligent American citizenhood, there is hereby established a society to be known as the 'Liberty Immigration Society.'"[23]

The second generation of immigrants was well represented in community affairs and members held a variety of public and political offices. Over the years there have been a number of state legislators whose parents came here as immigrants. They include members of the Fidel, Hanosh, Hindi, and Michael families. Others have served in law enforcement agencies, in the judiciary, and on state and county boards. Several families were especially prominent in the educational field.

Reluctance to integrate and assimilate was sometimes a defense mechanism used to counter discrimination in regions other than New Mexico. Numerous articles and official reports dealt with the undesirable character of Middle Eastern immigrants. Consular officials described the newcomers as lazy and dirty; peddling was seen as detrimental to dominant social mores—a way of avoiding a decent job and responsible lifestyle. It is likely that remarks and commentary like this forced newcomers to look inward, focus on their own community, and avoid contact with Americans. In the South, Arabic speaking immigrants were challenged in their citizenship applications, because they were not considered "white," while in nearby Oklahoma, an American educated Syrian doctor repeatedly complained in the Arabic press about the racial prejudice and social ostracism he encountered in his community.[24]

In New Mexico there is no evidence of any form of discrimination, except for a couple of isolated cases where the Syrians encountered prejudice on the basis of their religion and not their ethnicity. Descendants do not remember grandparents, parents, or other family members mentioning any kind of problem or opposition that they encountered from neighbors or the community as they settled in New Mexico. Occasionally, there were, of course, some misunderstandings over mundane affairs; when these occurred villagers referred to the immigrants as "turcos." Abe Peña in Grants verified this; he observed that Hispanic villagers customarily referred to the Syrians as "Los Árabes," except when they got mad and called them "turcos." But for the most part, he continued, the newcomers fit easily into their lives, and they did not find anything especially remarkable about them. "We were the farmers and they were the village merchants, who extended credit in times of need. They added a dimension to village life that I did not appreciate until later in life. We learned a little of their cooking, while they blended with our culture."[25]

To illustrate how well the Syrians became part of the community, Peña recalled an incident in his youth when someone asked about whether there were any gringos in San Mateo. One of the villagers replied that there were none and then reconsidered and said yes: there was actually one black man in the community.[26]

In summary, the assimilation of the Middle Eastern immigrants in New Mexico proceeded rapidly and with very few difficulties. Parents evidently did not insist on the continuation of Old World customs and mores; in many cases, they were not interested in preserving their native language. Efforts in later years by a few immigrants, like Raymond Shaya, for example, to teach children basic Arabic and some details about their background and culture came too late.

7

From Shopkeepers to Entrepreneurs

Through hard work and a frugal lifestyle many Syrian shopkeepers realized substantial savings that were either reinvested in their businesses or were used to branch out into other commercial ventures. Those with village stores customarily expanded their inventory and facilities. They were often the first to put money into the latest technologies, like radios, iceboxes, and telephones. Many also entered New Mexico's traditional industries of sheep, wool, and cattle, which required substantial investments in land and other materials. Syrian merchants in New Mexico towns, on the other hand, invested in real estate, the entertainment and early hospitality industry, in bars and in other endeavors. They became some of the state's most renowned entrepreneurs.

One of the first Syrian merchants in Albuquerque was Charlie Mama, listed also as Salim Mama Hyder, who was universally known for his frugality. A lifelong bachelor, he lived above his small store in the three hundred block of First Street across from the telegraph office. By 1910 or so he had saved enough money to send for his much young brother, Latif Mama Hyder (1900–1985), whom he enrolled in elementary school. Latif Hyder's classmate Karl Grundman remembered him as a painfully shy boy, who spoke no English. A few years later, Hyder was playing football at Albuquerque High School and would continue his studies at the University of New Mexico.[1]

By the late 1920s the brothers were already counted among major real estate investors in the city. They had bought land in the vicinity of the railroad that they sold at a large profit when the Santa Fe railroad decided to expand and needed that space. Local speculators were more than skeptical when the two brothers began to purchase thousands of acres of land on Albuquerque's arid west side. But convinced of the economic potential of New Mexico's largest city, they continued with their real estate acquisitions that would bring them a fortune in later years.[2]

In 1938 Latif Hyder built the popular Lobo Theater, the first movie theater outside of downtown. Four thousand people attended the opening to see *Old Chicago* with Tyrone Power and Don Ameche. One of the most loyal patrons of the theater was Hyder himself, who came almost nightly to watch the films being shown. He built an elegant villa in the southeast heights; close by the city laid out a public park on land that he donated and which bears his name.[3]

Agag M. Nassif was another prominent Syrian real estate magnate in the Duke City; unable to live in the humid Massachusetts climate, he arrived in New Mexico in the early 1920s. More commonly known as Joe Nassif, he may have been the only Syrian who came to the Southwest for health reasons.[4]

Surely the most outstanding Syrian entrepreneur in New Mexico was Nathan Salmon (or Solomon) of Santa Fe. Born in 1866 with the name of Na'aman Soleiman Farah to a trader and silk maker, he ran away from home and arrived in America in 1887—penniless and with very little formal education. Peddling brought him to the Southwest, and a massive snowstorm forced him to stay in Santa Fe in 1891, where he decided to settle after he had made fifty dollars in a pool game. He spent three years selling from a wagon in western New Mexico and in Navajo country. One of his more memorable experiences occurred one November evening in Durango, Colorado, where he overheard two men in the hotel lobby talking about killing a Thanksgiving turkey. Not familiar with American customs or with the English language, he was afraid that they were referring to him, so he barricaded himself in his room until he could leave the next day.[5]

Soon he had enough money to open a dry goods store in the city. This first mercantile business was so small that everyone called it the "wagon" store. But he quickly outgrew this space and began to buy adjacent property. Eventually he owned a whole block on San Francisco Street and built *The Emporium*, the largest and most modern store in the city. In 1913 he was elected president of the Santa Fe Retail Business Men's Association and headed the state organization two years later. (Salmon had applied for American citizenship in 1893, one of the earliest Syrian immigrants to do so.) By 1917 he was already so prominent in the community that historian Ralph Emerson

Twitchell included Salmon in *The Leading Facts of New Mexico*; Twitchell was especially impressed by Salmon's contributions to the community and by the quality of his merchandise. A similar laudatory description comes from Ellis Arthur Davis, who called Salmon one of Santa Fe's greatest benefactors in his *Historical Encyclopedia of New Mexico*.[6]

Nathan Salmon. Courtesy Alexis Koury Girard.

Nathan Salmon in his Santa Fe store. Courtesy Alexis Koury Girard.

In 1909 Salmon moved his family to an eight-bedroom home he had built on the corner of Don Gaspar and Paseo de Peralta. It was one of the finest houses in the city; vegetable gardens, orchards, a swimming pool, and several stables complemented the main building. His grandsons became avid polo players in later years. Encircling this estate was an elegant wrought iron fence that also framed an array of colorful tiles; on a trip south to Mexico Salmon had been impressed with the tile work and wanted to replicate the look in his own home. The family was known for its lavish and elegant parties that often included entertainment and the best china and linens available. On a more informal level, the home also hosted a lot of card games and belly dancing to Middle Eastern music.[7]

Salome Salmon, the family's only child, married E. John Greer in 1919; he had come to the United States in the early 1890s with his parents. His original name, Ar'ahb, was changed at Ellis Island to Greer. He had lost his father at a young age and was supporting his mother and siblings with a variety of jobs on the East Coast when he met his future wife. After their marriage, Greer joined the family business and in the 1930s the couple moved into the Salmon home that was large enough to accommodate their growing family.[8]

Before Salmon sold his mercantile business in the early 1920s to focus on real estate and other commercial ventures, he built two movie theaters—one was in Burro Alley and only featured Spanish language films and the other was the Paris Theater, which opened in 1914 and became the premier theater of the silent screen era. At the same time he built offices, parking garages, and other commercial buildings in Santa Fe, and in 1927 he erected the large Oden-Buick garage structure on North Fourth Street in Albuquerque.[9]

In 1930, Salmon publicized plans to build the largest theater in New Mexico. He wanted something that would demonstrate the latest technology in a setting that was unsurpassed at the time. The looming Depression evidently did not deter him, and on June 24, 1931, the Lensic Theater was opened with much fanfare and excitement. (The name for the theater comes from a combination of the first letter of each of his grandchildren's names.)[10]

Salmon had specified that he wanted something where magic happens; indeed, the Lensic Theater, designed by some of the most renowned architects of the time in Spanish-Moorish style, became the great cultural center of Santa Fe. The latest movies, vaudeville, and musical revues were shown there; Hollywood celebrities, like Judy Garland, Roy Rogers, and Errol Flynn attended openings. Guests were delighted with the sumptuous décor that included twinkling lights in the ceiling and one hundred leather rocking chairs in the mezzanine. Patrons could exit from the mezzanine to a dance hall next door; behind the theater Salmon erected a parking garage for 250 vehicles. Still visible at the entrance is a marble plaque that was installed at the opening and that reads: Dedicated to the People of Santa Fe by Nathan Salmon and E. John Greer. (After undergoing extensive renovations in the year 2000, the Lensic Theater is now included in the National Trust for Historic Preservation.)[11]

Lensic Theater in the 1930s. Courtesy Alexis Koury Girard.

The next spectacular venture for Salmon and Greer was the construction of the Hilton Hotel in Albuquerque. Salmon already had built the Plaza Hotel in Santa Fe and felt that the Duke City needed "something to keep the influential people with us, who have been passing through to California."[12] The ten-story Hilton Hotel was formally opened in June 1939; the two men financed its cost of six hundred thousand dollars. In attendance for the opening ceremony were two thousand people, including many local luminaries, like former governor Clyde Tingley; attorney W. H. Keleher; president of the Chamber of Commerce, Oscar Love; and Conrad Hilton, of course.[13]

Albuquerque Journal announces construction of Hilton Hotel in 1938.

It is clear that by the mid-1930s, Colonel Nathan Salmon was one of the wealthiest men in the state. In recognition of his outstanding services to New Mexico, two governors had appointed him Colonel Aide-de-Camp, and he liked to use that honorary title in later years. He also was issued a special license plate with the number one for many years. He had met Conrad Hilton shortly after he arrived in New Mexico when he used to spend the night at a boarding house run by Hilton's mother in San Antonio. Their friendship continued for many years and climaxed in 1942 when Hilton's second marriage to actress Zsa Zsa Gabor was celebrated in Salmon's lavish Santa Fe home. Unfortunately, Salmon had died a few months earlier and it was his son-in-law, John Greer, who hosted this memorable event.[14]

The Fidel brothers were also closely associated with the hotel industry. First to arrive in America was Joseph Fidel, who came from Roumieh a few years before World War I and was probably sponsored by an uncle living in Las Vegas since the early 1890s. Fidel and his cousin, Mack Rouckus, began as wagon peddlers in Union county.[15] (Rouckus later had a restaurant on

Albuquerque's First Street, called the Savoy Café. But he had to change the name to Depot Café, because the Savoy hotel next door did not like the use of its name. Rouckus's daughter became Latif Hyder's second wife.[16])

Mack Rouckus in the 1920s. Courtesy Harry Rouckus.

In the meantime, younger brother John, who was still in his teens and had been diagnosed with trachoma in Marseilles, sailed to Veracruz with plans to join his brother in Las Vegas. However, John Fidel first decided to try out business opportunities in northern Mexico, where he opened a small dry goods store with yard goods and notions. He also peddled part time with a donkey in tow. These were turbulent years in Mexico and Fidel dealt with a variety of crises: a landlord upset because the young peddler sold too much fabric to his wife; Pancho Villa's front man lounging in his store; and finally, an epidemic that threatened to close down the town. Eager to get out, Fidel collected outstanding accounts while puffing nonstop on a cigar that he hoped would kill germs. Henceforth, a lighted cigar became his trademark; he was rarely seen without one in his hands.[17]

John Nassar Fidel.
Courtesy LouDelle Fidel.

Both Fidel brothers started as peddlers and then opened a general merchandise store on Santa Fe's San Francisco Street and, shortly thereafter, a ready-to-wear business on the Santa Fe Plaza, where Woolworth would be located in later years. The elder brother, Joseph, left for Mount Lebanon to get married, but returned in the early 1920s with yet another brother, Toufic. Together the three brothers invested in a hay and grain business on Galisteo Street. Unfortunately, the advent of Prohibition adversely affected grain sales. But there were always other marketing possibilities. John Fidel told his daughter about a bootlegger who wanted to buy several bushels of rye in return for some whiskey. Several days later he delivered a barrel at the store and told Fidel to kick and roll the barrel often in order to cure the whiskey. After a time he returned to test the result. Fidel watched as he downed a healthy cup of liquid, but refused to pay right away, promising to do so in a couple of days. As he told his daughter in later years, "When he came back three days later, alive and not blind, I paid him."[18]

In spite of several mishaps, the first El Fidel Hotel, located in Santa Fe, was opened in 1925. It began two years earlier with several rooms that the brothers built on top of the feed store. "Gus the Greek" had suggested this expansion, because he promised to lease the second story as a hotel. A few months after completion, the sheriff warned the Fidels that, instead of a hotel, the upstairs premises were being used for gambling and that it had to be shut down immediately. A new investor was quickly on the scene. He had some experience with the Harvey Hotels and promised to lease the hotel if the Fidels built an annex behind with thirty additional rooms. A year later there were again problems and the brothers decided to run the hotel themselves.[19]

Like several other Syrian immigrants, the Fidels invested in the automobile business. Already in 1918 they acquired the Monitor Car Agency in Santa Fe with ten automobiles. This venture failed a short time later. Then they bought a Ford truck to use for their ongoing peddling. Returning from Albuquerque was always a special challenge; without a fuel pump, they had to ascend La Bajada in reverse, so that the gas flowed forward into the engine. In the late 1920s they bought a garage on Fifth and Copper in Albuquerque to service downtown hotels. They watched as a hotel project across the street failed and then decided to see if they could get the financing to continue with the construction. It seemed hopeless at first, but then John Fidel, with the help of banker Arthur Seligman in Santa Fe, floated his own bond issue and managed to procure sufficient finances to build the hotel, which was finally opened in 1931. With two hundred rooms the second El Fidel Hotel, in downtown Albuquerque, was the largest hotel in the state.[20]

In 1936, the Fidels enlarged the hotel with a second wing that included a large dance hall, La Sala Grande, where the Big Bands of the era performed on a regular basis. Radio station KOB was transferred from Las Cruces to the basement of the El Fidel, where it operated for the next five years. The hotel was a popular meeting place for the Syrian community well into the post–World War II period; periodically there were Middle Eastern banquets and social affairs, daily get-togethers in the coffee shop, and frequent card games in the back rooms. It was also the site for many statewide conventions and meetings; John Fidel's daughter, LouDelle, who, along with her brother, grew up in the hotel, remembers the annual Cattlemen's Conventions, when live cows were stalled in the lobby for the duration of the meetings.[21]

Postcard featuring El Fidel Hotel in Albuquerque, New Mexico. Courtesy Nancy Tucker.

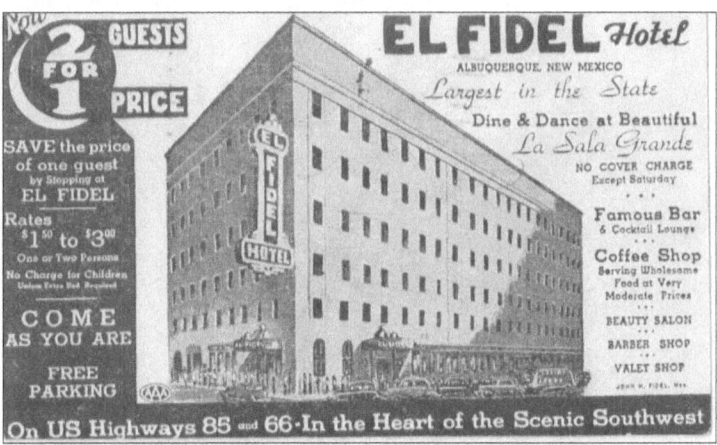

Promotional postcard of El Fidel Hotel in Albuquerque, New Mexico. Courtesy Nancy Tucker.

John and Toufic Fidel moved to Albuquerque to run the hotel, while Joseph stayed in Santa Fe. In the 1940s they bought the failing Meadows Hotel in Las Vegas and renamed it El Fidel. This hotel was put on the National Trust for Historic Preservation in 1983. In later years, John Fidel withdrew from the hotel business and invested in the oil industry. Another brother, Philip, emigrated in 1933 and managed the Santa Fe hotel for a brief time before World War II.[22]

In Las Vegas, New Mexico, brothers Obaid and George Maloof also opened a hotel. They had originally settled in Wagon Mound, but relocated to Las Vegas in the 1890s, where they operated several feed and general supply stores on Bridge Street. Obaid's real-estate holdings stretched down the south side of the street from the old fire station to 12th Street. Customers came via horse and wagon from various villages in northern New Mexico and were invited to store their horses and wagons in the barn the Maloofs built behind the store. Those who decided to spend the night in town were put up at the hotel for a special price. Aside from merchandising and real estate, the family bought a Buick agency and opened two theaters, the popular Kiva theater on Bridge Street and the Serf movie house. A number of cousins followed them—some settled in Las Vegas, others in Albuquerque and Bernalillo. There are several variations in the spelling of the last name.[23]

Obaid Maloof and children. Courtesy City of Las Vegas Museum. Frank Maloof collection.

Opening night at the Kiva theater in Las Vegas, New Mexico. Courtesy Palace of the Governors Photo Archives (NMHM/DCA), #66688.

The most exciting new entertainment business in the 1920s and 1930s was the movie industry. It had an almost universal appeal, especially since going to the cinema to see Hollywood films was something almost everyone could afford. Moreover, it was not difficult, or particularly expensive, to bring movies to outlying communities and villages. Therefore, it is not surprising that many Syrians, in addition to Nathan Salmon, the Maloofs in Las Vegas and Latif Hyder, opened movie theaters.

In Bernalillo both the Silva and the Abousleman families were involved in the movie business. James Silva bought some used equipment from Nathan Salmon and opened the Zia Theater. Some years later, when the city widened the road in front of the theater, its last few rows of seats were razed. Ron

Abousleman remembers his father and uncle tinkering with a portable screen and projection system that they carried to Jemez Springs, Cuba, and other villages in the area to show the latest Hollywood productions in halls that were rented for the occasion. The Tabets operated movie theaters in Mountainair and later Belen, while the Merhige and Fidel families did the same in Española.[24]

The end of Prohibition opened up new business possibilities and also brought to an end a few, but fairly well known, bootlegging ventures in the Syrian community. The Silvas in Bernalillo opened their saloon the day after Prohibition ended in 1933 and have been in operation ever since. In Albuquerque Azize Michael ran the popular nightspot, El Grande, for many years, while Joseph Budagher opened a bar on the highway between Albuquerque and Santa Fe. Syrian-owned drinking establishments opened in Belen, Mountainair, San Mateo, Bibo, Jemez Springs, Cerrillos, and other New Mexico communities, but the most profitable undertaking was Joe Maloof's purchase of the Budweiser distributorship for New Mexico and, a short while later, the Coors beer distributorship. This decision propelled the family into statewide commercial activities and from there into national prominence.[25]

Maloof building in Las Vegas, New Mexico. Photo by Monika Ghattas.

Other entertainment-related businesses engaged the community. The Tabets built a popular dance hall in Belen, and the Abouslemans promoted ice-skating and boxing in Bernalillo. Al Hurricane started his boxing career in Abousleman's Coronado Hall. The bathhouse in Jemez Springs, formerly located along the Jemez River south of its present location, was certainly unique among business ventures. Moses Abousleman bought the bathhouse in 1924 and remodeled it by installing new tubs and other modern facilities. Business was apparently quite good and people traveled considerable distances via horse and buggy on a dirt road up the canyon to bathe in the hot sulfur springs, hoping to cure or, at least, alleviate the pains of arthritis and rheumatism. Treatment for these ailments consisted of bathing daily in the springs for twenty-one consecutive days. With very little hotel space available, most people camped along the river. Years later, Abousleman's youngest son, Tom, ruefully remembered the many afternoons he had to spend in the bathhouse collecting entrance fees. Unfortunately, a flood in 1941 covered everything in mud, and only the family used the bathhouse intermittently after that disaster.[26]

The Bellamahs, another major entrepreneurial family, attained prominence not only in Albuquerque, but also in several cities in the Southwest. Najib Bellamah arrived in the territory of New Mexico in the early 1890s and worked with Merhige Michael peddling in central New Mexico. Like many other of his countrymen, he returned to Mount Lebanon to continue his education and eventually became the village schoolmaster. Around 1909 he returned with his young wife and finally settled in Albuquerque after World War I, where he enrolled his two young sons, Anise and Abdullah, in St. Michael's School. Both boys were fluent in Spanish and Arabic, but could not speak English. Bellamah opened a dry goods business in the Barelas neighborhood and, like other Syrian families in the city, socialized with the Italian community. Because of his educational background and his ability to speak several languages, Bellamah was much respected by his fellow countrymen and was often called upon to translate documents and write letters for them.[27]

Both of his sons became successful businessmen in later years. Anise partnered with a prominent Italian family to establish the statewide Southwest Distributing Company. His younger brother, known as Dale Bellamah, became a premier residential developer and was named the sixth largest national homebuilder in the 1950s. His Albuquerque subdivision, Princess Jean Park, was featured in several national publications, and one of his model homes is on display in the Smithsonian Institution as part of the Science in American Life Exhibit.

Najib Bellamah in the early 1900s.
Courtesy Patricia Bellamah Boyle.

Anise and Dale (Abdullah)
Bellamah in 1919. Courtesy
Patricia Bellamah Boyle.

Anise and Dale Bellamah in the 1930s. Courtesy Patricia Bellamah Boyle.

Related to one of Mount Lebanon's princely families, the Bellamahs made frequent trips to Lebanon in later years to check on their property. However, for their first return trip, they had to rely on their Younice relatives in Dixon to verify that they were born in the United States, since all records were destroyed in a church fire in Veguita.

Interestingly, one of the largest national clothing manufacturers had his beginning in New Mexico. Mansour Farah (ca. 1885–1937) is closely associated with El Paso, but he first came to New Mexico in 1905 from Biskinta, Mount Lebanon, via Canada. Why he chose New Mexico is not clear; most likely there was a relative or friend already here. He and his brother, Andrew, following the established custom, saved their earnings from peddling in the southern part of the state and then opened a feed and general store in Las Cruces, as well as the first movie theater in the community. But in 1920 Farah decided to become a tailor and left for New York to learn the trade. After his return, he started a small manufacturing company in El Paso that employed ten seamstresses for six sewing machines and made chambray cotton shirts. He rapidly expanded until Farah industries became one of the largest clothing manufacturers in the country, specializing in denim pants, khaki clothing, and other men's furnishings.[28] During the 1920s and 1930s there was also a George Farah in the clothing business in Truth or Consequences. He must have been a relative who moved away after a few years.[29]

Raymond Shaya of Santa Fe had one of the most unusual occupations for a Syrian immigrant. As an insurance agent for Mutual Life of New York, he traveled all over the state during his career. Acquainted with every Syrian family in the area, he assumed the role of informal liaison person in the community. Shaya left Mount Lebanon in 1909 as a fifteen-year-old. Because one of his companions spoke Spanish, they elected to go to Havana, where Shaya stayed for several months. The following year he went to Santa Rosa, New Mexico, where his sister and brother-in-law had settled. They had arrived in Las Vegas in the middle of the 1890s and peddled in the area for a while. But when the Chicago, Rock Island and Pacific Railroad built a line through Santa Rosa in 1902, they decided to move south and open a store in the new railroad town.[30]

Fluent in Arabic but without any knowledge of English, Shaya was very homesick and planned to return to Mount Lebanon after he had made a little money. His sister sent him to a local high school for a year and then he went to work for his brother-in-law with a starting salary of ten dollars a month. In 1916 he was hired as an agent for Mutual Life of New York. His weekly salary was more than the monthly wages he earned in the store. Three days before the end of World War I, he was inducted into the army; shortly thereafter, he received his citizenship.

Sixty years after starting in this profession, Shaya still marveled at his good fortune. He was only twenty-two years old when he became an insurance agent with a solid salary that widely surpassed his expectations. Similar to the ubiquitous Syrian peddlers, he was forced to assimilate quickly in his work. All of his early customers were Americans; his family and friends, on the other hand, were amused by the idea of buying life insurance. "What's that good for?" laughed his brother-in-law; others asked him why anyone would want to leave a lot of money to a wife—wouldn't she just use it to find another husband? Reflecting on these early years, Shaya remarked that most of his Syrian countrymen were suspicious of American institutions, like banks and insurance companies. They preferred to keep personal control of their money.

The insurance company brought him to Albuquerque, where he lived until 1933 when he was transferred to Santa Fe. As superintendent agent, he did a lot of traveling with his job, not only in the state, but also nationally to attend conventions and meetings. These experiences and his constant contact with the Anglo community gave him a unique perspective on American life, but also made him more aware of the values of his own culture.

Shaya was particularly concerned about the fact that he and his compatriots had neglected to teach their children something about their culture. For several years Shaya conducted Arabic lessons for the children in Santa Fe. (More than sixty years later James Koury still keeps his notebook of vocabulary and writing exercises on his office bookshelf.[31]) He also organized gatherings of the Syrian community in Santa Fe and Albuquerque and was instrumental in the founding of the Cedars of Lebanon Club, which met for several years. Asked about what he had brought with him from Mount Lebanon, he remarked that his most valued possession was an axiom his parents had instilled in him in his youth:

Whoever you are, be noble.
What you do, do well.
When you speak, speak kindly.
Give joy wherever you dwell.

In the 1940s Shaya served several terms on the Santa Fe City Council and was the Republican candidate for mayor in 1954. He lost by a few votes but continued his interest in city government for many years. He also opened a jewelry store and traveled to Lebanon several times. His one regret was that he never saw his parents again.

In conclusion, it is evident that these first-generation immigrants not only arrived in the Southwest with versatile skills, but they also did not hesitate to explore new business opportunities. It is also possible that New Mexico's nonindustrial environment was more conducive to entrepreneurship—the preferred means to success. Some scholars have maintained that many Syrian immigrants were "ready made Yankees" when they arrived, even though they were poor and had few resources. They wanted to own property as quickly as possible and participate in the American free-enterprise system.[32]

In New Mexico they were especially drawn to new and modern commercial ventures, like moving pictures, the nascent hotel industry, and the mushrooming automobile market. In many instances, the pursuit of these opportunities continued to be in context of the family.

8

The Women: Resilient and Resourceful

Immigration history has usually focused on men for obvious reasons. Paramount among these is the fact that many more men emigrated, and their success or failure determined the degree of family accommodation in the New World. The plight of women was rarely considered; it was assumed that their adjustments were less traumatic because many continued the familiar lifestyle of homemaking once the family was established in its new locale. This is, of course, true, but only in a limited context. Women also had to negotiate through the formidable challenges a new environment presented. They had to learn a new language and become familiar with a culture that often seemed puzzling, anomalous, and, at worst, threatening. Many have their own testimonials and experiences, and it is their stories that have received considerable attention in more recently published autobiographies and memoirs. These have provided a much more detailed and engaging portrait of these women and have enabled further studies, such as that of Evelyn Shakir, *Bint Arab: Arab and Arab American Women in the United States*.[1]

Women immigrants from Mount Lebanon shared many similarities with those who came from southern Europe and the Mediterranean area. They were young, often illiterate, and came to America with their husbands or followed them at a later time. They were by and large village women who knew little of the world outside of their immediate environment. However, it would be mistaken to think that they came from a sheltered environment, more commonly seen among urban and upper class women. Aside from their nurturing role, they were expected to contribute to the economic welfare of the family by selling their garden produce, bartering handicrafts in village markets, and carefully allotting family resources. The patriarchal character of village life did not limit their public role. In addition, many women in Mount Lebanon supported and cared for their families—sometimes for years—while their husbands were exploring economic opportunities in the New World.

Syrian immigrants included an unusually large number of women; in the decade before World War I women comprised about one-third of the newcomers. This figure increased to almost 50 percent in the immediate postwar period, before the enactment of immigration restrictions. These percentages were considerably higher than those of comparable ethnic groups, such as Spanish, Greek, or Armenian immigrants. It is possible that the assimilation of Syrian immigrants was expedited, in part, by the large number of family units that came to America. Families are incorporated into new communities more readily than individuals.[2]

Interestingly, a considerable number of married Syrian women came to the New World alone. Some traveled with friends, relatives, or neighbors, while others brought their children to begin a new life and left behind husbands who were reluctant to make a new start. Shakir relates many stories of women seeking adventure, escaping from a bad marriage, or deciding to act on an initiative that seemed dubious to other family members.[3] A famous example was the mother of poet Khalil Gibran, author of the perennial best seller, *The Prophet*. Unable to tolerate her husband's drinking any longer, she left with her four children for the New World. In New Mexico, a half-century after the fact, Adele Azar still marveled at her mother-in-law who arrived in southern Colorado with her four boys. When the expected help from her brothers did not materialize, she went on the road peddling until her youngest son became very ill and forced her to return home. Some years later her husband made his first journey to America with the much-improved son. He stayed and she refused to make another trip to America; they never saw each other again.[4]

As with other immigrant groups, a few of the women coming to New Mexico suffered considerable hardships and personal tragedies on their transatlantic voyages. For Latify Merhige it was the loss of her two oldest daughters. While she and her husband Fidel were preparing to emigrate, they entrusted the two older children to the paternal grandmother. On the day of embarkation, the grandmother did not show up with the two girls. She probably had become attached to them and hoped that keeping them with her would ensure the return of her son. (Apparently this was not an unusual occurrence.[5]) John Merhige, Latify's oldest son, who was born in New Mexico shortly after their arrival, recalled his mother's weekly telephone calls to speak with her daughters, whom she did not see again until forty years later when she made a return trip to Mount Lebanon.[6]

When Rose Ashkar Fidel arrived at Ellis Island in the early 1920s, she was not allowed to enter and had to return home. Her husband, Joseph Fidel, living in Santa Fe, had arranged immigration papers for his family of three to follow him. However, his infant daughter had died at sea and officials did not accept the discrepancy in numbers. There are other similar tales that include sick children detained at entry ports for unreasonable lengths of time and others who ran out of money and could not contact relatives.[7]

It would be difficult to draw a representative image of the Syrian women who came to New Mexico. Such an attempt could easily lead to distortion; but it is certain that they did not conform to what Margaret Sellers in her study has described as the false "stereotype of immigrant women built on an image of seclusion, a sheltered lifestyle and a total and exclusive dedication to family."[8] These kinds of perimeters would not have been functional in New Mexico for a variety of reasons. Given their small numbers and dispersion over a wide area, the women felt compelled to interact with the local community quickly and build a support system that would help them adjust to their new circumstances. Relying on fellow countrywomen for help and companionship was in most cases not a practical option. It also proved to be unnecessary since they encountered a culture and social system that permitted quick and easy acculturation.

Many of New Mexico's Syrian women performed a dual role: the traditional one of taking care of the family and the necessary one of helping husbands in the general store. Since many of the men continued peddling after they had invested in a business, the women often ran the stores during their absences. Those who did not work outside of the family were integrated into the community through their children. Several mothers evidently learned how to read and write in English when their children started school.

Commercial responsibilities were without doubt an important impetus in the rapid community integration of many Syrian women. They quickly learned Spanish to communicate with their customers and, more importantly, to socialize with their new neighbors. With little formal effort, they were drawn into the life of the village or neighborhood; they shared their neighbors' problems and their celebrations. Thus assimilation proceeded with few difficulties.

In a few instances the women became the principal family provider when their husbands died. Rafnaa Coury decided to stay in Duran, New Mexico, and continue the family business, even though her husband was killed by a band of outlaws there in the early 1920s. Likewise, Helima Maloof in Las Vegas operated a grocery store on Bridge Street for years after her husband, George, died prematurely and left her with three young sons to support.[9]

One of the most exceptional stories is that of Clara Merhige Sahd, described by her American daughter-in-law as a very strong woman who spoke a mixture of Arabic, English, and Spanish, except when she was angry and reverted to her native tongue. She was sixteen years old when she arrived in New Mexico to join her family in Española and Las Vegas. When she ran out of money in Chicago, she had to wire her uncle to send her enough for the rest of the railroad ticket. But when she finally arrived in Las Vegas, there was no one to pick her up; not familiar with the English language, she waited for more than twenty-four hours before someone appeared to take her home. A few years later Clara married a cousin, the former shoemaker Fittie Sahd, and the couple settled in Cerrillos. Unfortunately, Fittie died in the late 1930s, leaving Clara with five small boys to support in a closed company town. Incredibly resourceful and hard working, she asked the director of the coalmine, Oscar Huber, for permission to peddle in the surrounding mining communities. With a suitcase filled with novelties, linens, and clothing she went on the road selling her wares, usually with one of the older boys in tow. She alternated taking one of them out of school, so they could help her carry the merchandise. She even made contact with a Chicago firm that supplied her with ladies' apparel. In addition, she sewed curtains for the Civilian Conservation Corps and manufactured yard goods from chicken feed bags. But life was difficult and she finally decided to move north and go into business with her brothers in the Española area.[10]

Her two sons, Gabe and Jay Sahd, recalled an incident before Christmas that must have taken place shortly after their father died. To add a festive touch to the holidays, Clara decided to augment the traditional Christmas dinner with some tamales her friend, Clarita, made in Madrid. So she sent her two sons to Madrid to pick up the tamales. However, when they arrived, they were not ready, so they left to watch an ongoing baseball game in town. Hours later when they returned for the tamales, they still were not finished, so they walked around town looking at the Christmas lights, for which Madrid was well known. Late that evening the tamales were finally done and the two tired boys started back to Cerrillos. Meanwhile, Clara had become very concerned about her sons, but she had neither a car nor a telephone. So she begged a neighbor to drive her to Madrid; about halfway along the stretch she found her two boys trudging along the dark road. The next day she served her Christmas dinner, telling her boys that there were no presents this year, but that she had made the dinner especially nice for them.[11]

Edna Abousleman smoking water pipe in Jemez Springs, New Mexico. Courtesy Tom Abousleman.

Several of the women supervised large households that included the family as well as seasonal help, servants, and temporary lodgers. Edna Abousleman in Jemez Springs had a nine-bedroom house for her family of eight children. Indians from nearby Jemez Pueblo delivered a hundred wagonloads of wood every fall to heat this home. The Abousleman house was the first one to have electricity, running water, and a telephone. Villagers called her Doña Catalina and consulted her about herbs and remedies for injuries and complicated childbirth. She spoke three languages, but was illiterate. During the summer months her home was a social center for many Syrian families from the area, who came to picnic in the mountains, to visit, and bath in the springs.[12]

Another example of these remarkable women was Doña Meme of San Mateo. She married her childhood sweetheart, Merhige Michael, when he returned from his first trip to New Mexico and then followed him in 1909 with her oldest son Michael. The family settled in San Mateo after Merhige Michael bought a small business and expanded it into a general store. There Meme raised eleven children, helped her husband tend the store, and cooked gargantuan meals that gradually became a mixture of Arabic and New Mexican cuisine. Saturdays was baking day and Abe Peña, whose best friend was one of the Michael boys, still remembers the "gigantic Arabic tortillas" that came out of the oven. The former legislator Toby Michael, who was the oldest grandson, spent much time with his grandparents and recalled enormous evening meals that often included unexpected guests. There was an abundance of rabbits in the area in those years and Doña Meme always had thirty to forty frozen rabbits hanging on two fifty-foot clotheslines on the back porch in winter. With these she cooked a variety of dishes, cutting down a couple of them as more people arrived.[13]

What made the greatest impression on the community, however, was her prolific garden and adjacent orchard, something rarely seen in that area. This was her special pride, and villagers were amazed by the variety and amount of produce she grew every season. (One of her younger sons followed her example and ran a farmers' market in Grants for many years.) Her neighbors also were amused by the way she managed to hold her own against her strong-willed and authoritarian husband.[14]

Sallie Faris Budagher lived in Santo Domingo Pueblo for three years shortly after she married her husband. She evidently made such an impression on the people that they sang a song about her for years afterward. Santo Domingo was one of the more conservative pueblos and had seen difficulties with state and federal officials; in 1919 the only government official allowed on their land was an Indian agent appointed in Washington. This ban included all doctors with whom the Indians had had problems.[15] Thus during the years when she lived in the pueblo, Sallie Budagher acted as an intermediary between the mothers of sick children and doctors waiting outside pueblo land. She made detailed reports of symptoms and other critical health information and then brought back medicines and instructions on treatment. Since the Budaghers kept a large vegetable garden, she did a lot of canning and participated in communal food preparation. She introduced canned vegetables into the winter diets of Indian families and encouraged more variety in food choices. Evidently comfortable among the women, she defended them in domestic disputes and offered them a temporary shelter in her home. One of these women stayed with the family for years, even after the Budaghers moved out of the pueblo.[16]

Sallie Budagher. Courtesy *Viva El Pasado: A History of the Bernalillo Area (1973–74)*.

Obviously, the many similarities between life on Mount Lebanon and in rural New Mexico facilitated and eased the adjustment to a new life for many of these women. Probably half were illiterate, but they successfully negotiated between two different cultures. They learned Spanish, adopted local customs, and made homes for their families that retained some features of their background. Their descendants do not remember mothers or grandmothers overcome by grief or regret about the hardships they encountered. The majority were practical women, too busy to succumb to nostalgia. They adjusted well and established strong roots in their communities by engaging in church, village, and neighborhood activities; a few served on local school boards and were active in service and charitable organizations. None of them worked outside of the family; unmarried girls always lived and worked within the family unit. All together they distinguished themselves with their resiliency, adaptability, and remarkable courage.

Conclusion

It is undeniable that the Syrian traders and peddlers who arrived here in the late 19th century are characterized by their adaptability and their special skills as cross-cultural traders. Their ease in assimilating and their effortless integration into the culture and society of New Mexico were directly related to their background and to the unique conditions existent in this state

These Middle Eastern immigrants arrived in New Mexico not as a displaced peasantry, but as a people looking for economic opportunities. Their good fortune was to encounter a lifestyle and a culture that suited their skills and social values. In addition, the timing of their arrival was propitious; political, economic, and social conditions were in the process of being transformed by modern technologies, a new governmental system, and a gradual cultural reorientation towards the dominant Anglo population. These developments gave them unique opportunities to promote and participate in these ongoing changes. As first generation immigrants they distinguished themselves by readily assuming civic responsibilities and engaging in community activities.

Their quick assimilation enabled them to enter into their new communities more rapidly than was possible in other parts of the country. By dispersing throughout the state, they escaped the slums and exclusive ethnic neighborhoods that impeded assimilation and fostered prejudice. Most importantly, they did not progress from an immigrant group into an ethnic community. The continuation of a specific ethnic identity was never a priority among most of the immigrants. Consequently, a considerable number of third generation descendents have only a vague understanding of their ethnic background.

In reviewing the early Arab immigrant experiences in New Mexico, it becomes clear that there were three pivotal events that impacted their lives:

World War I, the growing anti-immigrant sentiment that culminated in the 1924 Johnson-Reed Immigration Act and finally the Depression. It was probably the Depression that had the most direct effect on several families in this state.

Immigration figures climbed steadily in the immediate pre-war period, both nation-wide and in New Mexico. This came to an end in 1914 when all trans-Atlantic travel came to a halt. Moreover, the war evidently forced some immigrants who had returned home for a visit to remain in Mount Lebanon for the duration of hostilities. In other cases, families were separated for five years, because the men had traveled ahead, but their wives could not follow as planned.

The war also offered unexpected benefits. Several young Syrians served in the armed forces and thereby earned American citizenship. By serving in the military they expedited their assimilation process and improved their command of the English language.

The growing anti-immigrant sentiments after the war must have been known in Mount Lebanon, because there was a sense of urgency about coming to America in the immediate post-war period. (The horrendous conditions in Lebanon during the war were another powerful impetus for emigration.) Starting with the 1921 Immigration Restriction Act, it became increasingly more difficult for people from the Middle East to enter this country. Three years later the passage of the Johnson-Reed Act virtually stopped immigration from that part of the world. Some Syrians continued to come through Mexico in the 1920s, but this was not a substantial number. Thus the majority of the Syrian families that settled in New Mexico came before World War I.

The Depression and the drought of the 1930s were difficult times. Rural economic conditions deteriorated dramatically, so that destitute villagers were unable to pay their outstanding accounts to Syrian shopkeepers, forcing some of them to move into towns. Many others, however, survived economic set backs and continued merchandising well into the post World War II period. By diversifying their investments they managed to overcome or, at least, weather adverse conditions.

Attracted by new technologies, a notable number of Syrian families became part of the general modernization and urbanization trends of the post-World War I period. Their entrepreneurial activities often extended to other areas of the state. Although their close association with the Hispanic community continued, the Syrians also forged closer ties to other ethnic groups, particularly to Italian and Greeks immigrants.

~~~

It is interesting to note that many Syrian immigrants maintained close ties to their homes and villages for years after they left. They continued to support family members and quite a few made a trip back to Mount Lebanon after they had retired. There is also a noticeable interest in the third generation to visit the homeland of their grandparents.

To their children the first immigrant generation bequeathed a strong emphasis on social responsibility, on family loyalty, and on the importance of education. They may have spoken wistfully at times of the parents they left behind, the customs and comforts of home they remembered, but they did not succumb to nostalgia. Pride in their heritage did not impede the affection and appreciation they held for their new homes.

The narrative of Los Árabes in New Mexico epitomizes the fulfillment of the American dream: economic wellbeing, upward social mobility, and the promise of seemingly unlimited opportunities. They shared the American middle class values of thrift, hard work, and perseverance and found in New Mexico a setting that rewarded ingenuity and encouraged individualism. They were not afraid to take risks and contributed to the economic and political development that marked the early twentieth century. Their presence enriched and enlarged the cultural and social parameters of their communities. They became proud citizens and gifted this state with their love of family, their unique culture and their boundless optimism.

It is hoped that this study will call attention to the presence of Los Árabes in New Mexico and highlight their contributions to the culture and history of this state. A study of this kind is never complete; hopefully, it will encourage descendents, sometimes reluctant to delve into the past for a variety of reasons, to come forward with more information to enhance and expand this narrative.

Notes

Introduction

1. See Robert Elliott Barkan, "Turning Turner on His Head? The Significance of Immigration in Twentieth-Century American Western History," *New Mexico Historical Review* 77, no. 1 (Winter 2002): 57–88. Barkan examines the role of smaller ethnic immigrant groups in the history of the West and mentions Croats, Finns, Armenians, Basques, and others that are often ignored, but he does not include Syrian immigrants.

2. Alixa Naff, *Becoming American: The Early Arab Immigrant Experience* (Carbondale: Southern Illinois Press, 1984), 4. Philip M. Kayal includes a detailed discussion of the many religious, regional, and political divisions of Arab Christians in the United States in "Arab Christians in the United States," Sameer Y. Abraham and Nabeel Abraham, eds. *Arabs in the New World: Studies on Arab-American Communities* (Detroit: Wayne State University Center for Urban Studies, 1983), 48–49.

3. Theodore Pulcini addresses the often problematic use of "Arab American" in contemporary writings and emphasizes that this designation refers to a shared linguistic and cultural background and not to national and/or political realities. Theodore Pulcini,"Trends in Research on Arab Americans,"*Journal of American Ethnic History* 12 (4): 27–60.

4. For an excellent discussion on this topic, see John Bodnar, *Remaking America: PublicMemory, Commemoration, and Patriotism in the Twentieth Century* (Princeton, NJ: Princeton University Press, 1992), chap. 3, "The Construction of Ethnic Memory."

Chapter 1

1. Valuable for general background information are: Charles Issawi, "The Historical Background of Lebanese Immigration, 1840–1914," in *The Lebanese in the World: A Century of Emigration*, ed. Albert Hourani and Nadim Shehadi (London: I. B. Tauris, 1993); Samir Khalaf, *Persistence and Change in 19th Century Lebanon* (Beirut: American University of Beirut, 1979); idem, "The Background and Causes of Lebanese-Syrian Immigration to the United States before World War I," in *Crossing the Waters: Arab-Speaking Immigrants to the United States before 1940*, ed. Eric J. Hoogland (Washington, DC: Smithsonian Institution Press, 1987), 17–37; Philip K. Hitti, *The Syrians in America* (New York: George H. Doran, 1924); idem, *A Short History of Lebanon* (New York: St. Martin's Press, 1965).

2. Hitti, *A Short History*, 194–97; William W. Harris, *Faces of Lebanon: Sects, Wars, and Global Extensions* (Princeton, NJ: Marcus Wiener Publishers, 1997), 107–9; Issawi, "Historical Background," 21.

3. Hitti, *A Short History*, 197; Hooglund, "Introduction," in *Crossing the Waters*, 5; Harris, *Faces of Lebanon*, 107–9.

4. Issawi, "Historical Background," 23–24; Hitti, *A Short History*, 189; Akram Fouad Khater, "'House' to 'Goddess of the House': Gender, Class, and Silk in 19th Century Mount Lebanon," *International Journal of Middle East Studies* 28, no. 3 (1996): 325–48; idem, *Inventing Home: Emigration, Gender, and Middle Class in Lebanon, 1870–1920* (Berkeley: University of California Press, 2001), 19–47.

5. Issawi, "Historical Background," 24; a good discussion about the modernization of Beirut is in Fawwaz Traboulsi, *A History of Modern Lebanon* (London: Pluto Press, 2007), 52–72.

6. Hitti, *A Short History*, 201.

7. Khalaf, "Background and Causes," 23.

8. An extensive examination of the Protestant presence in the Middle East is in Adele L. Younis, *The Coming of the Arabic- Speaking People to the United States*, ed. Philip M. Kayal (Staten Island, NY: Center for Migration Studies, 1995), chapters 2–5.

9. See Patricia Nabti, "Emigration from a Lebanese Village: A Case Study of Bishmizzine," in *The Lebanese in the World*, 43 and passim. Also, Younis, *The Coming of the Arabic-Speaking People*, 11–12, mentions how Europeans encouraged "Oriental Christians" to undermine Turkish hegemony, suggesting that they could not be Christians and Arabs at the same time. Philip M. Kayal in the introduction to the Younis book, page xiii, discusses how the Christian Maronites in particular were encouraged by the French to disavow their Arab origin and heritage—something that continues to contribute to the political instability of the area and may explain, in part, why many second-generation Syrian Christians, whose parents had come from Mount Lebanon, insist that they are not Arabs. Also, Eric J. Hooglund in the introduction to his book *Crossing the Waters*, page 7, points out that the term "Arab" customarily referred to a Muslim, especially to a Bedouin, during the late Ottoman period, and that the term "Syrian" may have come from European missionaries

10. Younis, *The Coming of the Arabic-Speaking People*, 71–72.

Chapter 2

1. Valuable for a recent analysis on immigration is Roger Daniels, *Coming to America: A History of Immigration and Ethnicity in American Life*, 2nd ed. (New York: HarperPerennial, 2002), 3–29. For information on Syrian immigration, see Khalaf, "The Background and Causes of the Lebanese-Syrian Immigration," 17–37; Najib Salibi, "Emigration from Syria," *Arab Studies Quarterly* 3 (1981): 5–24; Hitti, *The Syrians in America*; Naff, *Becoming American*, 76–128; Philip M. Kayal and Joseph M. Kayal, *The Syrian–Lebanese in America: A Study in Religion and Assimilation* (Boston: Twayne Publishers, 1975), 60–88; Gregory Orfalea, *Before the Flames: a quest for the history of Arab-Americans* (Austin: University of Texas Press, 1988), and Issawi, "The Historical Background."

2. Hitti, *The Syrians in America*, 48–49; Khater, *Inventing Home*, 13, maintains that it was not poverty, but rising expectations that propelled peasants to leave the mountains and emigrate.

3. Ed Aryain, *From Syria to Seminole: Memoir of a High Plains Merchant* (Lubbock: Texas Tech University Press, 2006), 38, recalls the steamship agents trying to recruit in Henna, a small village a few miles outside of Damascus; see also Hourani and Shehadi, *The Lebanese in the World*, 5; Naff, *Becoming American*, 91–100;

4. Hitti, *The Syrians in America*, 51.

5. According to Passport Canada, "The rising popularity of rail travel in the mid–19th century led to an explosion of tourism throughout Europe and caused a complete breakdown in the European passport and visa system. In answer to the crisis, France abolished passports and visas in 1861. Other European countries followed suit, and by 1914, passport requirements had

been eliminated practically everywhere in Europe. However, World War I brought renewed concerns for international security, and passports and visas were again required, as a 'temporary' measure."

6. Stories of oppression and exploitation in mountain villages are abundant in memoirs. See Elmaz Abinader, *Children of the Roojme: A Family's Journey* (New York: W. W. Norton, 1991); Amin Maalouf, *Origins: A Memoir*, trans. Catherine Temerson (New York: Farrar, Straus and Giroux, 2004); Raff Ellis, *Kisses from a Distance: An Immigrant Family Experience* (Seattle: Cune Press, 2007). Also valuable is Evelyn Shakir, *Bint Arab: Arab and Arab American Women in the United States* (Westport, CT: Praeger, 1997), who recorded many firsthand accounts.

7. E. Lee Francis II, interviewed by Monika Ghattas, March 1978; Ronald Abousleman, interviewed by Monika Ghattas, November 10, 2009; Rasmieh Hindi, interviewed by Monika Ghattas, September 9, 1994; Adele Azar, interviewed by Monika Ghattas, September 9, 1977. LouDelle Fidel, interviewed by Monika Ghattas, January 8, 2011.

8. Elizabeth Boosahda, *Arab-American Faces and Voices: The Origins of an Immigrant Community* (Austin: University of Texas Press, 2003), 19–22.

9. N.A., "Syrians in the United States." *Literary Digest* 61, no. 5 (1919): 43.

10. Valuable discussion on this theme is in David Lowenthal, *The Heritage Crusade and the Spoils of History* (Cambridge: Cambridge University Press, 1998), 75 and passim. See also Khalaf, "Background and Causes," 29.

11. John Bodnar, "The Construction of Ethnic Memory," in *Remaking America: Public Memory,Commemoration, and Patriotism in the Twentieth Century* (Princeton, NJ: Princeton University Press, 1992), 41–78; Naff, *Becoming American*, 13 and 86–90.

12. Khater, *Inventing Home*.

13. Kayal, *The Syrian-Lebanese in America*, 119–120, suggests that these immigrants may have sent more money per capita to their relatives than any other immigrant group; see also Younis, *The Coming of the Arabic-Speaking People*, 135; Abinader, *Children*, 5; Hitti, *A Short History of Lebanon*, 209; Thomas Caldwell, "The Syrian-Lebanese in Oklahoma" (master's thesis, University of Oklahoma, 1984), 13, describes how the Lebanese in Oklahoma looked upon their stay in this country as a temporary necessity to save money so that they could return home "to live a life of ease."

14. Naff, *Becoming American*, 70–80. Engin Deniz Akarli, "Ottoman Attitudes towards Lebanese Emigration, 1885–1910," in *The Lebanese in the World*, 111–12, passim.

15. Naff, *Becoming American*, 84.

16. Khalaf describes terrible conditions in villages during World War I in chapter 2 of his book, *Persistence and Change*; see also Hitti, *A Short History*, 215–17; Abinader, *Children*, 110–18, 150–51, passim; Issawi, "Historical Background," 23–26; and Salibi, "Emigration from Syria."

17. Naff, *Becoming American*, 114.

18. Oswaldo M. S. Truzzi, "The Right Place at the Right Time: Syrians and Lebanese in Brazil and the United States, a Comparative Approach," *Journal of American Ethnic History* 16, no. 2 (1997): 8; Kayal, *The Syrian-Lebanese in America*, 71.

19. Khater, *Inventing Home*, 62; Nebti, "Emigration from a Lebanese Village, 41–63. Naff, *Becoming American*, 95; Younis, *The Coming of the Arabic-Speaking People*, 127; Aryain, *From Syria to Seminole*, 17.

20. National Bureau of Economic Research, *Statistics*, vol. 1 of *International Migrations*, ed. W. F. Wilcox (New York: National Bureau of Economic Research, 1929), 384–88, as illustrated in Khalaf, "Background and Causes," Table 1, in Hoogland, *Crossing the Waters*, 20; Naff, *Becoming American*, 110–11.

21. Younis, *The Coming of the Arabic-Speaking People*, 152. Alixa Naff included a photograph of the exposition in her juvenile edition of *The Arab Americans* (Philadelphia: Chelsea House Publishers, 1999.) Displayed are all kinds of ornate vessels, jeweled daggers, carpets with Oriental motifs, inlaid tables and similar merchandise.

22. See the website of the US Department of State, Office of the Historian, for more information.

23. Naff, *Becoming American*, 108–111; Truzzi, "The Right Place," 14.

24. Naff, *Becoming American*, 102–3; also see Roberto Marín Guzmán, "Los inmigrantes árabes en México en los siglos XIX y XX: Un estudio de historia social," in *El mundo árabe y América Latina*, ed. Raymundo Kabchi (Mexico City: J. Nacif Mina en colaboración con el Instituto Cultural Mexicano Libanés, 1995), 123–53; Nebti, "Emigration from a Village," 137.

25. "Seraphic Report re Conditions on the Mexican Border," National Archives Immigration File No. 51423-1, p. 14, as quoted in Sarah E. John, "Arabic-Speaking Immigration to the El Paso Area, 1900–1935," in Hoogland, *Crossing the Waters*, 107.

26. For a descriptive and thorough account of these border crossings, see Theresa Alfaro-Velcamp, *So Far from Allah, so Close to Mexico: Middle Eastern Immigrants in Modern Mexico* (Austin: University of Texas Press, 2007), 31–44, 53–55, 95–97; Sarah Elizabeth John, "'Trade Will Lead a Man Far': Syrian Immigration to the El Paso Area, 1900–1935" (master's thesis, University of Texas at El Paso, 1982), 24–43, also relates similar information.

27. Alfaro-Velcamp, *So Far from Allah*, 33–43; John, "Trade Will Lead a Man Far," 24–43; titled "Masters of Mendicants," *New York Times*, February 21, 1888, sec. 3, labels Middle Eastern immigrants as an 'infestation of cities' that form syndicates of beggars and peddlers. They are shiftless and their women have bold, dark eyes in comparison to the earnest, honest faces of the Swedes. In 1924 they are described as undesirable and lazy immigrants who do not get naturalized at the same rate as northern Europeans, *New York Times*, February 17, 1924, sec. 8. Together with the Chinese and Italians, they enter the United States illegally through Mexico, *New York Times*, June 17, 1923, sec. 2, and January 3, 1924, sec. 2. The negative stereotyping of Syrian immigrants is covered in Kayal, *The Syrian-Lebanese in America*, 90–94.

28. Guzmán, "Los inmigrantes," 130. According to Kobei Hashimoto, "Lebanese Population Movements, 1920–1939, in *The Lebanese in the World*, 97, there were between 250–300 Syrians in El Paso by the late 1920s.

29. Hooglund, *Crossing the Waters*, 11; Kayal, *The Syrian-Lebanese in America*, 72.

30. See Kayal, *The Syrian-Lebanese in America*, chap 6–9, for a thorough discussion on the role and significance of religion and churches in the lives of the Syrian immigrant community.

31. See Tomas Jaehn, *Germans in the Southwest, 1850–1920* (Albuquerque: University of New Mexico Press, 2005), chap. 1, "The Hispanic Southwest in German Literature," for a detailed discussion on the German interest in the Southwest. It is also noteworthy that some of the earliest descriptions and sketches of Albuquerque in the Albuquerque Museum of Art and History were done by German travelers in this area. Balduin Müllhausen published *The majordomo: A tale from Southern California and New Mexico* in 1863, and four of Rudolf Cronau's drawings of Albuquerque, done in the 1880s for a German publication, hang in the museum vestibule.

32. State naturalization records are found in *Naturalization Records by New Mexico Courts, Vol. I: Loose Documents (1852–Forward)*, extracted and compiled by Karen Stein Daniel and Elizabeth Louise Allright (New Mexico Genealogical Society, 2005); *Naturalization Records by New Mexico Courts, Vol. II: Docket Books (1867–1929)*, extracted and compiled by Karen Stein Daniel (New Mexico Genealogical Society, 2007); *Colorado Genealogical Chronicles*, vol. 37, Denver Federal Archives (Lakewood, CO: Foothills Genealogical Society of Colorado, 1998), 18; *Thirteenth Census of the United States Taken in the Year 1910* (Washington, DC: Department of Commerce, Bureau of the Census, Government Printing Office, 1913) indicates that there are 140 from Turkey in the territory of New Mexico, 176–82. These figures are probably more accurate than

those listed by Richard R. Greer in a 1942 article in the *New Mexico Historical Review*, where he lists one person from Turkey in 1880 and in 1890 and seventeen in 1910. Richard R. Greer, "Origins of the Foreign Born Population of New Mexico during the Territorial Period," *New Mexico Historical Review* 17, no. 4 (1942): 284.

33. *Naturalization Records, Vol. II*, 188, 230–31.

34. Judith Boyce DeMark, "The immigrant experience in Albuquerque, 1880–1920" (PhD dissertation, University of New Mexico, 1984), 69 and 78.

35. *Twelfth Census of the United States, 1900*. Socorro, New Mexico; Roll: T623; Precinct No. 2.

36. *Naturalization Book, Vol. II*, 216, lists Naguib Bellamah; Patricia Bellamah Boyle, linterviewed by Monika Ghattas, summer 2009; *The Twelfth Census of the United States, 1900*: Census Place: Hot Springs, Bernalillo, New Mexico; Roll: T623, lists Abousleman family, Simon Michael, and Younis (Unes) family. *Thirteenth Census of the United States, 1910*: Census Place: Peña Blanca, Sandoval, New Mexico; Precinct no. 12, includes Tanous Freye.

37. Alexis Koury Girard, interviewed by Monika Ghattas, June 3, 2009.

38. Younis, *The Coming of the Arabic-Speaking People*, 193; Adele Azar interview; Philip Maloof, interviewed by Monika Ghattas, October 8, 2010.

39. James Koury, interviewed by Monika Ghattas, November 11, 2008; Younis, *The Coming of the Arabic-Speaking People*, 166.

40. See www.encyclopedia for an explanation of the *partido* system.

41. Charles Ilfeld Company Records, Copybook #36, letter of Max Nordhaus to Hugo Goldenberg, February 18, 1896; letter of Charles Ilfeld to Rafael Mendes, March 24, 1896.

42. Ibid. Copybook #47, letter of Charles Ilfeld to Meyer Friedman, May 4, 1898.

Chapter 3

1. Naff, *Becoming American*, 128. This is the most exhaustive study on Arab peddling, esp. chapters 4 and 5, 128–60. Kayal, *The Syria- Lebanese in America*, 91, describe peddling as the key to the Syrian-Lebanese Americanization process, even though it also brought them much disdain. Also useful are Shakir, *Bint Arab*, part 1: The First Wave, 1875–1925, 13–76; Gregory Orfalea, "There's a Wire Brush in My Bones," in Hooglund, *Crossing the Waters*, 173–85; and Daniels, *Coming to America*, 206–9.

2. See, for example, Ed Aryain, *From Syria to Seminole*; Amin Maaloof, *Origins: A Memoir*; Elmaz Abinader, *Children of the Roojme*; Raff Ellis, *Kisses from a Distance: An Immigrant Family Experience*; Abrahim Mitri Rihbany, *A Far Journey* (Boston: Houghton Mifflin, 1914), describes his dislike of peddling on pp. 198–99.

3. William Peter Blatty, *i'll tell them i remember you* (New York: W. W. Norton, 1973), 16–17.

4. Daniels, *Coming to America*, 207.

5. Naff, *Becoming American*, 193–98.

6. Louise Seymour Houghton, "Syrians in the U.S.," *Survey* 26 (July–September 1911): 481–95, 647–65, 787–803; *Survey* 27 (October 1911): 957–68. Critical commentary about Arab peddlers is in Lucius Hopkins Miller, "A Study of the Syrian Communities in Greater New York," *Federation: Quarterly of the Federation of Churches and Christian Organizations in New York City* 3.2 (October 1903): 13–57, as quoted in Shakir, *Bint Arab*, 39–40.

7. Alice E. Christgau, *The Laugh Peddler* (New York: Young Scott Books, 1968).

8. Adele Azar interview; Brahaim Hindi, interviewed by Monika Ghattas, July 27, 2008; Alexis Koury Girard interview; Philip Maloof interview.

9. Naff, *Becoming American*, 169.

10. Nasario García, *The Naked Rainbow and Other Stories* (Albuquerque: University of New Mexico Press, 2009), 130.

11. Photocopy of page 181, September 24, 1891, Nicolla [sic] Abdalla paid three dollars to E. V. Chavez, Probate Clerk, for peddler's license #864. This transaction is duly notated by C.A. Robinson, Sheriff and collector of Socorro County. Author received photocopy from Nick Abdalla.

12. Paula Francis Allen and E.Lee Francis,"Yo cruso siete mares," *Confluencia* 1, no. 2 (1976): 19.

13. Ellis Arthur Davis, ed., *Historical Encyclopedia of New Mexico*, vol. 1 (Albuquerque: New Mexico Historical Association, 1945), 621.

14. This was mentioned by several descendants, including A.Samuel Adelo, Adele Azar, John Amin, Theodore Sahd, and E. Lee Francis.

15. Naff, *Becoming American*, 172; Shakir, *Bint Arab*, 36.

16. Conversation with Ken Wells, May 12, 2009.

17. Alvaro-Velcamp, *So Far from Allah*, 30.

18. Arthur L. Campa, "Hispanic Culture," 53–55, as quoted in Marta Weigle and Peter White, *The Lore of New Mexico* (Albuquerque: University of New Mexico Press, 2003), 295.

19. Harvey Fergusson, *The Conquest of Don Pedro* (New York: William Morrow, 1954).

20. Weigle, *The Lore of New Mexico*, 296–97; Reyes N. Martinez, "Gypsy Caravans," NMFWP, May 7, 1937, WPA-5-5-2 #19, H-MNM.

21. Charles Ilfeld Company Records, Copybook #36, Letter of Max Nordhaus, February 18, 1896; see also William Parish, "The German Jew and the Commercial Revolution in Territorial New Mexico, 1850–1900, " *New Mexico Historical Review* 35 (April 1960): 129–143.

22. William Parish, *The Ilfeld Company: A Study of the Rise and Fall of Mercantile Capitalism in New Mexico* (Cambridge, MA: Harvard University Press, 1961). Parish quotes from a letter he received from H. P. Stapp in Las Vegas on August 14, 1950, 393.

23. Casimira Delgado, "Who Were These Gypsies?" *La Herencia* 18 (Summer 1998): 27.

24. Lou Sage Batchen, "Los Pedlers," NMFWP, April 21, 1941, WPA-5-5-49 #50, H-MNM.

25. Reyes N. Martinez, "Arabs and Dancing Bears," NMFWP, May 1, 1937, WPA-5-5-47 #1, H-MNM.

26. Lorenzo de Córdova, *Echoes of the Flute* (Santa Fe: Ancient City Press, 1972), 14.

27. García, *The Naked Rainbow*, 121–36. Also, letter of Nasario García to Monika Ghattas, March 2009.

28. K. D. Stoes, "Peddlers in the Old Frontier," *New Mexico Magazine* (February 1951): 22–50.

29. *Cuentos: Tales from the Hispanic Southwest*, selected and adapted in Spanish by José Griego y Maestas; retold in English by Rudolfo A. Anaya (Santa Fe: Museum of New Mexico Press, 1980), 82–85.

30. The story about the US Camel Corps is included in many Southwest histories; most recently, Gary Nabhan devoted a whole chapter, titled "Camel Whisperers," to this entertaining episode in *Arab/American: Landscape, Culture, and Cuisine in Two Great Deserts* (Tucson: University of Arizona Press, 2008), 9–28.

31. Odie B. Faulk, *The U.S. Camel Corps: An Army Experiment* (New York, Oxford University Press, 1976), 107 & 174; J. Marvin Hunter, "Camel Driver's Son was President of Mexico," *Frontier Times* 19, no. 1 (October 1941), 1–2.

32. Naff, *Becoming American*, 168–82; Shakir, *Bint Arab*, states that one-third of the peddlers in the East were women, 38. See also Houghton, "Syrians in the US," part 2, 650; *Al-Hoda*, July 14, 1903, 2.

33. John, "'Trade Will Lead a Man Far,'" 62.

34. Gabriel and Jay Sahd, interviewed by Monika Ghattas, December 12, 2008, and March 2009. This story is also included in Patricia L. Sahd and Theodore M. Sahd, eds., *The Sahd Family Recipes: An American Feast Lebanese Style* (1986), 9–10.

35. E. Lee Francis II interview, and E. Lee Francis IV, interviewed by Monika Ghattas, August 2008 and February 5, 2009.

36. Ibid.

37. Naff, in *Becoming American*, interviewed some of the original generation. The general optimism and lack of despair are also evident in the other studies and memoirs mentioned earlier.

38. Nasario García, ed., *Comadres: Hispanic Women of the Río Puerco Valley* (Albuquerque: University of New Mexico Press, 1997), 33.

39. John Amin, interviewed by Monika Ghattas, December 2, 2009.

Chapter 4

1. However, it is noteworthy that New Mexico was the least urbanized state in the West. In 1920 Albuquerque was the largest town with a population of 15,000. Walter Nugent, "The People of the West Since 1890." In *The Twentieth Century in The West*. Gerald D. Nash & Richard W. Etulain, eds. (Albuquerque: University of New Mexico Press, 1989): 46–45.

2. Joseph Fidel, interviewed by Monika Ghattas, August 31, 2010; Ray Peña, interviewed by Monika Ghattas, February 2009.

3. Telephone conversation with Ted Sahd, March 2009.

4. Information about the Tabet family is a composite of the following interviews: Gloria Tabet Trujillo, interviewed by Monika Ghattas, October 1, 2008; Louise Tabet, telephone interview by Monika Ghattas, July 10, 2008; Renee Tabet, interviewed by Monika Ghattas, January 2009; Viola Sanchez, interviewed by Monika Ghattas, November 2009; Alice Tabet Sanders, telephone interview by Monika Ghattas, January 2010.

5. *Twelfth Census of the United States, 1900*; Census Place: Lincoln, Lincoln, New Mexico: Roll: T623_1001; Page: 2A; Enumeration District: 64. Ancestry.com. 1900 US Census.

6. Wesley R. Hurt, *Manzano: A Study of Community Disorganization* (New York: AMS Press, 1989), 80. This book is based on the author's thesis written in 1935: Wesley R. Hurt, "Manzano: A Study of Community Disorganization" (master's thesis, University of New Mexico, 1935). Although identical in many parts, the thesis includes a few more details pertinent to this study.

7. *Naturalization Records by New Mexico Courts, Vol. II*, 289. Juan Tabet was the father of Alice Tabet Sanders, telephone interview by Monika Ghattas.

8. *Naturalization Records by New Mexico Courts, Vol. II*, 289.

9. *Manzano Marriages, December 1854 through December 1913*, extracted, translated, and formatted by Louis Gilberto Padilla y Baca (Albuquerque, N.M., 2003), 99. Telephone interview with Louise Tabet.

10. *Fourteenth Census of the United States, 1920*: Census Place: Manzano, Torrance, New Mexico, Roll T625. Ancestry.com. 1920 US Census.

11. See note 5 above. Hurt, *Manzano*, 80.

12. Hurt, "Manzano" (thesis), 95.

13. Hurt, *Manzano*, 81.

14. Ibid, 82.

15. Valencia County Historical Society, *Rio Abajo Heritage: A History of Valencia County* (Belen, New Mexico: The Society, 1983), 238. Also see obituary of Frank Tabet, *Albuquerque Journal*, June 4, 1998, and obituary of Carlos Tabet Jr., *Albuquerque Journal*, December 12, 2000.

16. Hurt, "Manzano," 201.

17. Viola Sanchez interview.

18. Information on the Hindi family comes from: Brahaim Hindi interview; Rasmieh Hindi interview; Irene Ferris, interviewed by Monika Ghattas, April 28, 1978; Adele Azar interview. Also see Howard Bryan, "Off the Beaten Path," *Albuquerque Journal*, August 17 and 18, 1977. Rasmieh Hindi and her son, Moneer, are pictured in Brent Ashabranner, *An Ancient Heritage: The Arab-American Minority* (New York: HarperCollins, 1991), 28.

19. Alejandro Abraham Hindi, stock raiser, born in 1892 and in the United States in 1910, filed a Declaration of Intention in 1922, together with his wife, Clarita, born in 1897. *Naturalization Records, Vol. II*, 301. Milhelm Hindi filed a Declaration of Intention in 1913. He is listed as an unmarried peddler living in Las Vegas. *Naturalization Records, Vol. II*, 301. This declaration was canceled in 1919, because he did not file a Certificate of Arrival. *Naturalization Records by New Mexico Courts, Vol. I*, 129. The youngest brother, Amin Hindi (b. 1904), received American citizenship in 1934. *Naturalization Records, Vol. I (Loose Documents, Torrance County, 1882–1955)*, Collection #1959-281, Box #15780, 132.

20. For a recent article on the Hindi family and their Arabian horses, see Tim Keller, "Arabian Wind," *Western Horsemen* (September 2011): 76–79.

21. Information on the Anton Coury family comes from: Brahaim Hindi interview; Carol Darr, interviewed by Monika Ghattas, November 11, 2008; Raymond Shaya, interviewed by Monika Ghattas, April 27, 1978; Adele Azar interview.

22. *History of Torrance County* (Estancia, New Mexico: Torrance County Historical Society, n.d.), 131.

23. Robert J. Tórrez, *Myth of the Hanging Tree: Stories of Crime and Punishment in Territorial New Mexico* (Albuquerque: University of New Mexico Press, 2008), 48–49.

24. Information on the Salome family comes from the following interviews: Clara Salome Fidel, interviewed by Monika Ghattas, April 25, 1975; Jill Salome, interviewed by Monika Ghattas, November 4, 1998; Jeanette Salome Atencio, telephone interview by Monika Ghattas, February 4, 2009; *Fourteenth Census of the United States, 1920*; Census Place: Socorro, New Mexico, Roll: T625. Ancestry.com. 1920 Census.

25. This store unfortunately closed in 2008 after almost one hundred years in operation.

26. Anne Sullivan, "Magdalena's Salome Store—Doorway to the Past," *Southern New Mexico Travel and Tourism Information*, 1–2; Joel H. Bernstein, "Magdalena's Salome Store: A Living Link to Cowtown Days," *New Mexico Magazine* 77 (April 1999): 66–67.

27. Fred Salome is included in Ellis Arthur Davis, ed., *The Historical Encyclopedia of New Mexico*, vol. 2 (Albuquerque: New Mexico Historical Association, 1945), 1533. Also *Naturalization Records, Vol. II*, 301, notes that he filed a Declaration of Intention in 1920.

28. Nick Abdalla, interviewed by Monika Ghattas, May 12, 2009. *Thirteenth Census of the United States, 1910*; Census Place: Lemitar, Socorro, New Mexico, Roll: T624_918.

29. The author has a copy of these notations.

30. Author has a copy of this undated letter signed by Uncle Charlie. *Naturalization Records, Vol. II*, 301, has notation of Mikhail Shaheen or Chahin, merchant in Magdalena. Nick Abdalla interview; *Fourteenth Census of the United States. 1920*, Census Place: Magdalena, Socorro, New Mexico, Roll: T625, lists George and Adel Goze.

31. Davis, *Historical Encyclopedia*, vol. 2, 1676; Jacky Barrington, ed., *Magdalena: Celebrating One Hundred Years of Frontier Living* (Magdalena, New Mexico: Magdalena Old Timers' Association, 1984), 148; *Fourteenth Census of the United States, 1920*, Census Place: Magdalena, Socorro, Precinct 12; see ancestry.com. 1920 Census.

32. John Amin interview; Irene Abousleman Ferris interview.

33. Fayez Fandey, telephone interview by Monika Ghattas, January 6, 2011. E-mail correspondence with LaRena Miller, director, Geronimo Springs Museum in Truth or Consequences, December 29 and 30, 2010.

34. Abe Peña, *Memories of Cíbola* (Albuquerque: University of New Mexico Press, 1997), 186–90.

35. Information on the Francis family comes from the following sources: E. Lee Francis II interview; E. Lee Francis IV, interviewed by Monika Ghattas, August 2008 and February 5, 2009; Abelicio Peña. Paula Francis Allen and E. Lee Francis, "Yo cruso siete mares," *Confluencia* 1, no. 2 (1976): 14–22. The arrival of Elias Abu Hassan (Elias Francis) is notated in *Naturalization Records, Vol. II*, 230. See also the *Twelfth Census of the United States 1900*; Census Place: Cebolleta, Valencia, New Mexico; Roll: T623_1003, page 1A; see ancestry.com. 1900 census.

36. Peña, *Memories of Cibola*, 2.

37. E. Lee Francis II interview.

38. Anna Nolan Clark, "Mothers of Cebolleta," *New Mexico Magazine* 15 (February 1937): 17–19 and 39–40.

39. Nasario García, ed., *Comadres: Hispanic Women of the Río Puerco Valley* (Albuquerque: University of New Mexico Press, 1997), 41–43; Clark, "Mothers of Cebolla," 17–19.

40. García, *Comadres*, 33. Fruit orchards did not exist. Arab fruit vendors brought peaches, apricots, apples, and grapes to the area.

41. Abelicio Peña interview; Peña, *Memories of Cíbola*, 187.

42. Paula Gunn Allen, "Paternity," *Shadow Country* (UCLA Publication Services Department, 1982), 91–92; Other references to her extended family are in the following poems: Paula Gunn Allen, "Life Is a Fatal Disease," 45–46, and "High Steppin' Seboyetano," 25–26, *Life Is a Fatal Disease: Collected Poems, 1962–1995* (Albuquerque: West End Press, 1997).

43. Allen and Francis, "Yo cruso siete mares," 14 and passim; E. Lee Francis IV interview.

44. Clark, "Mothers of Cebolla," 40.

45. Comment by Ethel Gottlieb Francis during interview of E. Lee Francis II.

46. E. Lee Francis II showed citizenship document to author in 1978.

47. Joseph Hanosh, interviewed by Monika Ghattas, December 1977. All three Hanosh brothers are notated in *Naturalization Records, Vol. II*, 312 and 323.

48. Lance Robbins, "Trading Post, Hotels: Threads in Fabric of Immigrant's Life," *Albuquerque Journal*, November 11, 1979, Section F, 1 and 2. See also Davis, *Historical Encyclopedia o f New Mexico*, vol. 2, 1861.

49. Information on the A. H. Fidel family comes from: Joseph Fidel interview; Abelicio Peña interview; Toby Michael, interviewed by Monika Ghattas, October 2009 and June 30, 2010; Article in Grants' *Cibola Beacon* of December 31, 2009, featuring Joseph Fidel, Person of the Decade; Fidel's arrival in New York in 1913 is notated in *Naturalization Records, Vol. II*, 313, under his original name, Fadel.

50. For the image of the Route 66 postcard featuring Fidel Curio Store, see the Burton Frasher Postcard Collection housed in the Pomona Public Library, California. See *Albuquerque Journal*, October 29, 2009, for information about the historic site listing.

51. Information on the Merhige Michael family comes from: Toby Michael interviews; Abelicio Peña interview; Peña, *Memories of Cibola*, 186–89.

Chapter 5

1. Steve Armenta, "Cerrillos: A Story of Survival, " *La Herencia* 18 (Summer 1998): 22–23. The effect of the railroad on the state's economy has been covered in many articles; see, for example, G.L. Seligman, Jr., "The El Paso and Northeastern Railroad's Economic Impact on Central New Mexico, *New Mexico Historical Review 61*, no. 3 (July 1986): 217–231.

2. Rasheed Michael's 1898 petition for citizenship is notated in the *Colorado Genealogical Chronicles*, vol. 37, 18; his arrival in 1888 is listed along with E. Lee Francis in *Naturalization Records by New Mexico Courts, Vol. II*, 230. Sahd, *The Sahd Family Recipes*, 6–7, 13; Jay Sahd, interviewed by Monika Ghattas, December 9, 2008.

3. Sahd, *Family Recipes*, 8–9; Jay Sahd interview; Theodore Sahd, interviewed by Monika Ghattas, July 30, 2010.

4. *Worley's Directory of Albuquerque, New Mexico, 1909–10* (Dallas: John F. Worley Directory Co., 1909). The directory lists four to five Syrian dry goods stores in the city.

5. Helen Michael Azar, interviewed by Monika Ghattas, May 13, 2009; *Worley's Directory of Albuquerque New Mexico, 1904* (Dallas: John F. Worley Directory Co., 1904), 129. Azize Michael's petition for citizenship in 1900 is noted in *Colorado Genealogical Chronicles*, vol. 37, 22.

6. Helen Michael Azar interview; Toby Michael interview.

7. Geraldine Snow, interviewed by Mo Palmer, photo archivist, The Albuquerque Museum of Art and History, 1990s; *Thirteenth Census of the United States, 1910*; Sandoval County, Precinct no. 12, lists Fares, Said, merchant, age thirty-three, born in 1877 in Syria and in New Mexico in 1904.

8. Saith Budagher, interviewed by Monika Ghattas, April 25, 1978; Emma Budagher Hindi, interviewed by Monika Ghattas, June 5, 2009; Rose Budagher Morris, interviewed by Monika Ghattas, spring 2010; Southwest History Class, *Viva El Pasado: History of the Bernalillo Area* (Bernalillo, New Mexico: Bernalillo High School, n.p., 1974–75), 179–84; *Thirteenth Census of the United States, 1910*; Census Place: Jemez Springs Sandoval, New Mexico, Roll T624-918, page 6A, notes Budagher living with his cousin. *Fourteenth Census of the United States, 1920*; Census Place: Santo Domingo, Sandoval, New Mexico; Roll T625-1079, page 8B, lists Budagher family residing in the pueblo.

9. Saith Budagher interview; Emma Budagher Hindi interview; Rose Budagher Morris interview.

10. Leo Crane, *Desert Drums: The Pueblo Indians of New Mexico, 1540–1928* (1928; repr., Glorieta, New Mexico: Rio Grande Press, 1972), 159–80; Saith Budagher interview; *Viva El Pasado*, 181–82.

11. Crane, *Desert Drums*, 250–52; Saith Budagher interview.

12. Saith Budagher interview; Emma Budagher Hindi interview.

13. Ibid.
14. Rose Budagher Morris interview; *Viva El Pasado*, 183; Lionel Rael, conversation with Monika Ghattas, February 17, 2011.
15. Rose Budagher Morris interview; Emma Budagher Hindi interview.
16. Antoinette Silva, interviewed by Monika Ghattas, December 3, 2008 and January 7, 2009; Rudolph Montoya, interviewed by Monika Ghattas, December 2009; *Viva El Pasado*, 209–12.
17. A pamphlet included in the CD case summarizes the events of this case; conversation with Lionel Rael.
18. Antoinette Silva interview.
19. James Koury interview; A. Samuel Adelo, interviewed by Monika Ghattas, November 16, 2008, and telephone interview, Summer 1980.
20. *Twelfth Census of the United States, 1900*; Census Place: Hot Springs, Bernalillo, New Mexico, Roll: T623_999, p.28. Tom Abousleman, interviewed by Monika Ghattas, May 18, 1993 and August 21, 2008; Irene Abousleman Ferris interview; Linda Vozar Sweet, "The Sky's the Limit for Jemez Pioneers," *New Mexico Magazine* (May 1997): 22–25; for photographs of the family, see Kathleen Wiegner and Robert Borden, *Jemez Springs* (Charleston, NC; Chicago, IL; San Francisco, CA: Arcadia Publishing, 2009), 23–24, 31–32, 38, 103–104.
21. Tom Abousleman interview. Vozar, "The Sky's the Limit," 25.
22. Tom Abousleman interview; Marian Sotel, interviewed by Monika Ghattas, September 9, 2008.
23. Tom Abousleman interview; Marian Sotel interview.
24. Tom Abousleman interview.
25. Ronald Abousleman interview.
26. Marian Sotel interview; Tom Abousleman interview.
27. *Twelfth Census of the United States, 1900*; Census Place: Albuquerque, Bernalillo, New Mexico; Roll: T623_999; Page: 13B, precinct 12, registered Tobias and Gabriel Younis as peddlers; Tobias Younis and family are pictured in Arnold Vigil, "New Mexico's Lebanese Influence," *La Herencia* (Fall 2003): 16; A. Samuel Adelo interview; Theodore Sahd interview; Patricia Bellamah Boyle interview; Rudolph Montoya interview.
28. A. Samuel Adelo interview; Ana Pacheco, "Abdallah Samuel Adelo," *La Herencia* (Spring 2004): 20–21. A.S. Adelo, "Ode to Pecos," *La Herencia*, Fall 1998, 29; Arnold Vigil, "New Mexico's Lebanese Influence," *La Herencia*, Fall 2003, 16–17.
29. A. Samuel Adelo interview; Samuel Adelo, "Santa Fe, Pecos, and a Bit of Lebanon," in John Pen La Farge, *Turn Left at the Sleeping Dog: Scripting the Santa Fe Legend, 1920–1955* (Albuquerque: University of New Mexico Press, 2001), 263–67; the harmonious relationship between New Mexico's Jewish wholesale merchants and the Syrian peddlers (and later shopkeepers and merchants) is summarized in an article by Noel Pugach, "New Mexico's Merchant Jews: Another Perspective," *Legacy* (March 2009): 2–3, 7. Pugach's information comes from the reminiscences of A. Samuel Adelo.
30. A. Samuel Adelo interview.
31. Ibid.
32. A. Samuel Adelo interview; *Santa Fe New Mexican*, November 10, 1977; Debra Hughes, "Mom & Pop Stores Offer Slice of Hospitality," *New Mexico Magazine* (November 1997): 36–38.
33. See discussion on this in Adelo, "Santa Fe," 263.
34. *Santa Fe New Mexican*, November 10, 1977.

35. A. Samuel Adelo interview.

36. Joseph Fidel, his wife Josephine, and their children are listed in the 1920 US Census for San Miguel County, New Mexico; the Hanosh business in Mora was featured in the *Albuquerque Journal*, November 11, 1979; a photograph of John and Rose Fidel is in Toby Smith, "Arrows from Strong Bows," *New Mexico Magazine* 60, no. 2 (1982): 20–27.

37. John Merhige interviewed by Monika Ghattas, May 16, 2000; *Albuquerque Journal*, April 9, 1999.

38. John Merhige interview; conversation with Robert Tórrez, summer of 2008.

39. A letter about the Colorado church is in the author's possession.

40. *Albuquerque Journal* (Business Outlook), October 27, 2005; Agnes Jane Sahd MacKaron, telephone interview by Monika Ghattas, August 17, 2010; Virginia Macaron Nassif, telephone interview by Monika Ghattas, August 18, 2010.

41. Susan Toothman, "From Zahle to Springer," *The Trader* (July 25, 1979), p. 2, 7 & 8.

42. See article in the *Albuquerque Journal*, April 20, 2011, "Tiny New Mexico Town Altered Archaeology." Also, a grave marker in Raton cemetery lists him born in Lebanon in 1875 and died in Raton in 1953.

43. See Wikipedia for information on Philmont Scout Ranch.

44. Adele Azar interview; Philip Maloof interview; search Colfax County, New Mexico, for early families, A–L.

Chapter 6

1. "Yo soy mexicano, casi" was a comment by one of the sons of Merhige Michael; his childhood friend, Abe Peña, recorded it. This remark is also on the back cover of Peña's book, *Memories of Cibola*; Abe Peña interview.

2. Michael Suleiman, "The Mokarzels' Contribution to the Arab-Speaking Community in the United States," *Arab Studies Quarterly* (March 22, 1999): 8–12 and passim. Also see Eric J. Hooglund, ed., *Crossing the Waters*, 7–8, and Kayal, *The Syrian-Lebanese in America*, chaps. 7–9.

3. John G. Bourke, "Notes on the Language and Folk Usage of the Rio Grande Valley (With Special Regard to Survivals of Arabic Customs)," *Journal of American Folklore* 9, no. 33 (1896): 81–116. University of Illinois Press on behalf of the American Folklore Society.

4. Marta Weigle and Peter White, *The Lore of New Mexico* (Albuquerque: University of New Mexico Press, 2003), chap. 10, 363–64, 382–90, and passim describe village social customs and the importance of rites of passage. For a description of Lebanese village life in the nineteenth century, see Khalaf, *Persistence and Change*, chap. 7.

5. E. Lee Francis II interview.

6. Hitti, *The Syrians in America*, 24–25; Michael W. Suleiman, "Early Arab Americans: The Search for Identity," in Hooglund, *Crossing the Waters*, 37–54.

7. Lowenthal, *The Heritage Crusade*, 61.

8. See Robert W. Larson, *New Mexico's Quest for Statehood, 1846–1912* (Albuquerque: University of New Mexico Press, 1968), 147–68, for detailed description of Hispanic attitudes in territorial period; also Robert J. Rosenbaum, *Mexicano Resistance in the Southwest* (Dallas: Southern Methodist University Press, 1998), 6 & 27.

9. For the role of religion in territorial New Mexico, see Rosenbaum, *Mexicano Resistance*, 9–11.

10. See Daniels, *Coming to America*, 267–68, and 275 for more details about the Catholic Church, and Kayal, *The Syrian- Lebanese in America*, 139–46, 158–59, and passim; Larson, *New Mexico's Quest*, 147–68, details problems about attaining statehood.

11. E. Lee Francis II interview; Toby Michael interview; Rosenbaum, *Mexicano Resistance*, 10 and 27.

12. "It was family honor and solidarity that was emphasized by my parents more than any other value," remembered John Merhege. John Merhege interview.

13. Sarah Deutsch, *No Separate Refuge: Culture, Class, and Gender on an Anglo-Hispanic Frontier in the American Southwest, 1880–1940* (New York: Oxford University Press, 1987), 9–10.

14. Eliseo "Cheo" Torres with Timothy L. Sawyer Jr., *Curandero: A Life In Mexican Folk Healing* (Albuquerque: University of New Mexico Press, 2005), 31–32, 10–11; Meldrum K. Wylder, *Rio Grande Medicine Man* (Santa Fe: Rydal Press, 1958), 116; Weigle, *The Lore of New Mexico*, 328–35; James Koury interview; Tom Abousleman interview; Sam Adelo interview; E. Lee Francis interview.

15. Torres, *Curandero*, 31–32, 10–11; Brahaim Hindi interview. Khalaf, *Persistence and Change*, 137; Sam Adelo interview; Tom Abousleman interview.

16. Fray Angélico Chávez, *My Penitente Land: Reflections on Spanish New Mexico* (Albuquerque: University of New Mexico Press, 1974), xiv; another interesting comment is on page 271, "because of our remote and more general theme, of the utmost interest were some few alliances with modern Jews, and later also Syrians and Lebanese. But even when there was no intermarriage at all, there has always been a more brotherly rapport with these people, as if blood were calling to blood from loin and landscape beyond memory's recalling. As remarked in passing many ages ago, in our Palestinian landscape some Hebraic folk found the opportunity to own open grazing land on which to enjoy raising sheep and cattle after centuries of ghetto living elsewhere in the world. In the long run, landscape and language were the final arbitrators in every phase of mores and customs."

17. For more examples, see: Marcello Sabatino, "The Arabic Element in Spanish," *The Arab World* (January–February 1963); A. Samuel Adelo, "Influence of Arabic in the Spanish Language" (typewritten paper, n.d.); Habeeb Salloum, "Arabic Contributions to the Spanish Language," in internet search.

18. Nabhan, *Arab/American*, 29–45.

19. Tibo Chavez, *New Mexico Folklore of the Rio Abajo* (Portales, New Mexico: Bishop Printing, 1972), 2; Nabhan, *Arab/American*, 35, 37–45; Rachel Laudan, "The Mexican Kitchen's Islamic Connection," *Saudi Aramco World* 55, no. 3 (2004). She discusses how Mexican cooking, including moles, stews, and many other dishes and spices have Moorish roots; N.A., "Trigo Cocido con Carne de Cabrito," NMFWP, June 1939, WPA5-5-24 #6, H-MNM.

20. Helen Azar interview; Patricia Bellamah Boyle interview.

21. A. Samuel Adelo interview; Raymond Shaya interview; Patricia Bellamah Boyle interview; E. Lee Francis II interview.

22. E. Lee Francis II interview; E. Lee Francis IV interview.

23. The quoted material was taken from a plaque that hung in the home of E. Lee Francis II. This organization may have been related to a committee, called "Freedom of Immigration," founded by Naoum Mokarzel around 1904, to persuade U.S. officials that Syrians and Lebanese were Caucasians. Mokarzel was the editor of *Al-Hoda*, the leading Arab newspaper. *Al-Hoda, 1898–1968: The Story of Lebanon and Its Emigrants as taken from the Newspaper Al-Hoda* (New York: Al Hoda Press, 1968), 7.

24. John, '"Trade Will Lead a Man Far,"' chap. 2; Suleiman, "Early Arab-Americans," in Hooglund, *Crossing the Waters*, 37–55; Raouf Halaby, "Dr. Michael Shadid and the Debate over Identity in

the *Syrian World*," in Hooglund, *Crossing the Waters*, 55–69; Nancy Faires Conklin and Nora Faires, "'Colored' and Catholic:' The Lebanese in Birmingham, Alabama," in Hooglund, *Crossing the Waters*, 70–85.

25. Abe Peña interview; Gloria Tabet Trujillo interview.

26. Abe Peña interview.

Chapter 7

1. Violet Grundman, interviewed by Monika Ghattas, July 6, 1999. Irene Abousleman Ferris interview. *Albuquerque City Directory*, 1909–1910, 191.

2. Irene Abousleman Ferris interview.

3. For information on the Lobo Theater, check internet. The younger of Latif Hyder's sons, Charlie Hyder, an astrogeophysicist, received considerable international publicity in the 1980s when he fasted for seven months in Lafayette Park, fronting the White House, to protest nuclear weapons and the Waste Isolation Pilot Plant in Carlsbad, New Mexico.

4. Virginia Macaron Nassif, telephone interview by Monika Ghattas, August 18, 2010; Irene Ferris interview.

5. Ralph Emerson Twitchell, *The Leading Facts of New Mexico History*, vol. 4 (Cedar Rapids, IA: Torch Press, 1917), 54–55. Davis, *Historical Encyclopedia of New Mexico*, vol. 1, 621; "Into the Fabric of Santa Fe: The Salmons and the Greers," *The Santa Fean Magazine*, vol. 6, no. 4 (1978): 15–18.

6. Twitchell, *The Leading Facts*, 54–55; "Into the Fabric", 15–16; Davis, *Historical Encyclopedia*, vol. 1, 621; *Albuquerque Journal*, June 9, 1939.

7. Sam Adelo interview; Alexis Koury Girard interview. In the 1980s the Salmon-Greer home was converted into The Club of Santa Fe, hosting elegant functions for the community.

8. "Into the Fabric, "18. Davis, *Historical Encyclopedia*, vol.1, 393.

9. *Albuquerque Journal*, June 9, 1939; Alexis Koury Girard interview.

10. For more information on the Lensic theater, check internet.

11. Ibid; "Into the Fabric," 17.

12. *Albuquerque Journal*, June 9, 1939.

13. Ibid.

14. Alexis Koury Girard interview; "Into the Fabric," 16–17; Nathan Salmon is also listed among biographies of the New Mexico Office of State Historians.

15. Rose Fidel, interviewed by Monika Ghattas, December 12, 2008; James Koury interview; LouDelle Fidel, interviewed by Monika Ghattas, January 8, 2011; Davis, *Historical Encyclopedia*, vol. 1, 631.

16. Harry Rouckus, interviewed by Monika Ghattas, January 27, 2011.

17. LouDelle Fidel interview.

18. Ibid.

19. Ibid.

20. Ibid.; Davis, *Historical Encyclopedia*, vol. 1, 631.

21. LouDelle Fidel interview.

22. LouDelle Fidel interview; Davis, *Historical Encyclopedia*, vol. 1, 447. Rose Fidel interview.

23. Sources on the Maloof family include: Philip Maloof interview; Sam Adelo interview; Mary Jean Maloof Koury, telephone interview by Monika Ghattas, December 10, 2008; *Naturalization Book*, #2, 11 and 115–116; *Fourteenth Census of the United States, 1920*; Census Place: Las Vegas, San Miguel, New Mexico; Roll T625_1079, 1A, lists 13 people with the surname of Maloof in San Miguel County, plus 13 more with the surnames of Malouff and Melouff; Arnold Vigil, "New Mexico Lebanese Influence," *La Herencia*, February 2003; *The New Mexican*, July 30, 2000, E–3; some family information is on Joe and Gavin Maloof's website.

24. Antoinette Silva interview; Ronald Abousleman interview; Philip Maloof interview.

25. Toby Michael interview; Philip Maloof interview.

26. Ronald Abousleman interview; Tom Abousleman interview; Linda Vozar Sweet, "The Sky's the Limit for Jemez Pioneers," *New Mexico Magazine* (May 1997): 22–25.

27. Patricia Bellamah Boyle interview; *Naturalization Book*, #2, 216, states that Najib Bellamah was born in 1877 and came to the United States as a minor in 1892. *Thirteenth Census of the United States, 1910*; Census Place: Albuquerque Ward 3, Bernalillo, New Mexico: Roll T624_913; page: 7B, lists Najib Bellamah, born in 1875, age thirty-five, from Turkey, as a literate peddler. His wife, Moheepa, is noted as born in 1891 and in New Mexico in 1909.

28. Alixa Naff, "Lebanese Immigration into the United States: 1880 to the Present," in Hourani, *The Lebanese in the World: A Century of Emigration*, 148; for a brief family and business history, see the *El Paso Times* website and the El Paso History Museum website.

29. John Amin interview; LeRena Miller, e-mail, December 28, 2010.

30. Raymond Shaya interview.

31. James Koury interview.

32. Kayal, *The Syrian-Lebanese in America*, 94–95; Sarah E. John, "Arab-Speaking Immigration to the El Paso Area, 1900–1935," in Hooglund, ed., *Crossing the Waters*, 109–111.

Chapter 8

1. Shakir, *Bint Arab*; see also Gregory Orfalea, "There's a Wire Brush in My Bones," in Hooglund, *Crossing the Waters*, 173–87; Evelyn Shakir, "Good Works, Good Times: The Syrian Ladies' Aid Society in Boston, 1917–1932," in Hooglund, *Crossing the Waters*, 133–47. Naff also includes many references to women in *Becoming American*, 167–79, 274–76, 283–88, and passim. Other valuable sources are *Al-Hoda* and the *Syrian World*, newspapers that regularly discussed topics pertinent to Syrian women, such as the changing mores of life in America, marriages among different sects, women peddlers, and so forth.

2. Hitti, *The Syrians in America*, 58; Naff, *Becoming American*, 111, 115–16.

3. Shakir, *Bint Arab*, especially chap. 4, 27–34.

4. Adele Azar interview.

5. Shakir, *Bint Arab*, 25.

6. John Merhige interview.

7. Rose Fidel interview.

8. Maxine Sellers, "Beyond the Stereotype: A New Look at the Immigrant Women, 1830–1924," *Journal of Ethnic Studies* 3 (1975): 59–70, has found that especially Middle Eastern women should not be stereotyped as illiterate and staying within four walls.

9. Carole Darr interview; Adele Azar interview; Mary Jean Maloof Koury interview.

10. Jay Sahd interview; Gabriel Sahd and Jay Sahd, interviewed by Monika Ghattas, May 11, 2009.

11. Jay Sahd interview; Gabriel Sahd and Jay Sahd interview.

12. Tom Abousleman interview.

13. Toby Michael interview. Abe Peña notes the abundance of rabbits in the area in an article in *La Herencia*, "Los Conejos de San Mateo" (Summer 2002). Abe M. Peña, *Villages and Villagers* (Los Ranchos de Albuquerque: Rio Grande Books, 2007), 71–72, has a chapter on *conejos*.

14. Toby Michael interview; Abe Peña interview; Peña, *Memories of Cibola*, 96.

15. Emma Budagher Hindi interview; Saith Budagher interview; Crane, *Desert Drums*, 242 and 245; *Viva El Pasado*, 179–84. Author has a printed copy of the information that pertains to the Joseph and Sallie Budagher family, given to her by Saith Budagher.

16. For information on abuse of women in the pueblo, see Crane, *Desert Drums*, 243–55. Emma Budagher Hindi interview; Rose Budagher Morris interview.

Bibliography

Abbreviations:

CSWR
Center for Southwest Research
University of New Mexico
Albuquerque, New Mexico

NMFWP
New Mexico Federal Writers' Program
Fray Angélico Chávez Memorial Library
New Mexico History Museum
Santa Fe, New Mexico

Archival Materials:

Batchen, Lou Sage. "Los Pedlers," NMFWP, April 21, 1941. WPA-5-5-49 #50. Fray Angelico Memorial Library, New Mexico History Museum, Santa Fe, New Mexico.

Charles Ilfeld Company Records, Copybook #36, letter of Max Nordhaus to Hugo Goldenberg, February 18, 1896; letter of Charles Ilfeld to Rafael Mendes, March 24, 1896. CSWR, University of New Mexico.

Martinez, Reyes N. "A Knight of the Grip," NMFWP, June 12, 1937. WPA-5-5-60 #6. Fray Angelico Memorial Library, New Mexico History Museum, Santa Fe, New Mexico.

———. "Arabs and Dancing Bears," NMFWP, May 1, 1937. WPA-5-5-47 #1. Fray Angelico Memorial Library, New Mexico History Museum, Santa Fe, New Mexico.

———. "Gypsy Caravans," NMFWP, May 7, 1937. WPA-5-5-2 #19. Fray Angelico Memorial Library, New Mexico History Museum, Santa Fe, New Mexico.

N.A. "Trigo Cocido con Carne de Cabrito," NMFWP, June 1939. WPA-5-5-24 #6. Fray Angelico Memorial Library, New Mexico History Museum, Santa Fe, New Mexico.

Official Documents and Published Sources:

Albuquerque City Directory and Business Guide [1896–1907]. Compiled by Hughes and McCreight. Albuquerque, New Mexico: Albuquerque Daily Citizen.

Colorado Genealogical Chronicles 37. Denver Federal Archives. Lakewood, CO: Foothills Genealogical Society of Colorado, 1998.

Fourteenth Census of the United States, 1920. Washington, D.C.; National Archives and Records Administration, 1920. T 625.

Hudspeth's Directory Company's Albuquerque City Directory [1915–1924]. El Paso, Tex.: Hudspeth Directory Company, 1915–1924.

Manzano Marriages, December 1874 through December 1913. Extracted, translated, and formatted by Louis Gilberto Padilla y Baca. Albuquerque, New Mexico, 2003.

Naturalization Records by New Mexico Courts, I: *Loose Documents (1852–Forward). Extracted and* compiled by Karen Stein Daniel and Elizabeth Louise Albright. Albuquerque, New Mexico: New Mexico Genealogical Society, 2005.

Naturalization Records by New Mexico Courts, 2: *Docket Books (1867–1929).* Extracted and compiled by Karen Stein Daniel. Albuquerque, New Mexico: New Mexico Genealogical Society, 2007.

New Mexico State Business Directory Including El Paso Texas, with Denver and foreign classifications. Denver: The Gazetteer Publishing and Printing Company, 1921.

Thirteenth Census of the United States, 1910. Washington, D.C.; National Archives and Records Administration, 1910. T 624.

Twelfth Census of the United States, 1900. Washington, D.C.; National Archives and Records Administration, 1900. T 623.

Worley's Directory of Albuquerque, New Mexico [1908–1917]. Dallas: John F. Worley Directory Co., 1908–1917.

Worley's Directory of Albuquerque New Mexico, 1904. Dallas: John F. Worley Directory Co., 1904.

Interviews:

Nick Abdalla, interviewed by Monika Ghattas, May 12, 2009.

Ronald Abousleman, interviewed by Monika Ghattas, November 10, 2009.

Tom Abousleman, interviewed by Monika Ghattas, May 18, 1993 and August 21, 2008.

A. Samuel Adelo interviewed by Monika Ghattas, November 16, 2008; telephone interview, summer 1980.

John Amin, interviewed by Monika Ghattas, December 2, 2009.

Jeanette Salome Atencio, telephone interview by Monika Ghattas, February 4, 2009.

Adele Azar, interviewed by Monika Ghattas, September 16, 1977.

Helen Michael Azar, interviewed by Monika Ghattas, May 13, 2009.

Patricia Bellamah Boyle, interviewed by Monika Ghattas, summer 2009.

Saith Budagher, interviewed by Monika Ghattas, April 25, 1978.

Carole Darr, interviewed by Monika Ghattas, November 11, 2008.

Fayez Fandey, telephone interview by Monika Ghattas, January 6, 2011.

Irene Abousleman Ferris, interviewed by Monika Ghattas, April 28, 1978.

Clara Salome Fidel, interviewed by Monika Ghattas, April 25, 1975.

LouDelle Fidel, interviewed by Monika Ghattas, January 8, 2011.

Joseph Fidel, interviewed by Monika Ghattas, August 31, 2010.

Rose Fidel, interviewed by Monika Ghattas, December 12, 2008.

E. Lee Francis II, interviewed by Monika Ghattas, March 1978.

E. Lee Francis IV, interviewed by Monika Ghattas, August 2008 and February 5, 2009.

Alexis Koury Girard, interviewed by Monika Ghattas, June 3, 2009.

Violet Grundman, interviewed by Monika Ghattas, July 6, 1999.

Joseph Hanosh, interviewed by Monika Ghattas, December 1977.

Azize and Moneer Hindi, conversation with Monika Ghattas, December 2011.

Emma Budagher Hindi, interviewed by Monika Ghattas, June 5, 2009.

Brahaim Hindi, interviewed by Monika Ghattas, July 27, 2008.

Rasmieh Hindi, interviewed by Monika Ghattas, September 9, 1994.

Mary Jean Maloof Koury, telephone interview by Monika Ghattas, December 10, 2008.

James Koury, interviewed by Monika Ghattas, November 11, 2008.

Agnes Jane Sahd MacKaron, telephone interview by Monika Ghattas, August 17, 2010.

Philip Maloof, interviewed by Monika Ghattas, October 8, 2010.

John Merhige interviewed by Monika Ghattas, May 16, 2000.

Toby Michael, interviewed by Monika Ghattas, October 2009 and June 30, 2010.

LaRena Miller, email correspondence, December 29 and 30, 2010.

Rudolph Montoya, interviewed by Monika Ghattas,December, 2009.

Rose Budagher Morris, interviewed by Monika Ghattas, spring 2010.

Virginia Macaron Nassif, telephone interview by Monika Ghattas, August 18, 2010.

Abelicio (Abe) Peña, interviewed by Monika Ghattas, February 1, 2009.

Lionel Rael, conversation with Monika Ghattas, February 17, 2011.

Harry Rouckus, interviewed by Monika Ghattas, January 27, 2011.

Jay Sahd, interviewed by Monika Ghattas, December 9, 2008.

Gabriel and Jay Sahd, interviewed by Monika Ghattas, March 2009.

Theodore (Ted) Sahd, interviewed by Monika Ghattas, July 30, 2010; telephone conversation, March 2009

Jill Salome, interviewed by Monika Ghattas, November 4, 1998.

Viola Sanchez, interviewed by Monika Ghattas, November 2009.

Alice Tabet Sanders, telephone interview by Monika Ghattas, January 2010.

Raymond Shaya, interviewed by Monika Ghattas, April 27, 1978.

Antoinette Silva, interviewed by Monika Ghattas, December 3, 2008 and January 7, 2009.
Marian Sotel, interviewed by Monika Ghattas, September 9, 2008.
Louise Tabet, telephone interview by Monika Ghattas, July 10, 2008.
Renee Tabet, interviewed by Monika Ghattas, January 2009.
Gloria Tabet Trujillo, interviewed by Monika Ghattas, October 1, 2008.

Newspapers:

Albuquerque Journal, June 9, 1939.
Albuquerque Journal, August 17 and 18, 1977.
Albuquerque Journal, November 11, 1979.
Albuquerque Journal, June 4, 1998.
Albuquerque Journal, April 9, 1999.
Albuquerque Journal, December 12, 2000.
Albuquerque Journal: Business Outlook, October 27, 2005.
Albuquerque Journal, October 29, 2009.
Albuquerque Journal, April 20, 2011.
Al-Hoda, July 14, 1903.
Cibola Beacon (Grants, New Mexico) of December 31, 2009.
New York Times, February 21, 1888.
New York Times, June 17, 1923.
New York Times, January 3, 1924.
New York Times, February 17, 1924.
The Santa Fe New Mexican, November 10, 1977.
The Santa Fe New Mexican, July 30, 2000.

Published Memoirs and Commemorative Publications:

Abinader, Elmaz. *Children of the Roojme: A Family's Journey*. New York: W. W. Norton, 1991.

Adelo, A.Samuel. "Ode to Pecos." *La Herencia* 19, Fall 1998, 29.

———. "Santa Fe, Pecos and a Bit of Lebanon." In John Pen La Farge. *Turn Left at the Sleeping Dog*. Albuquerque: New Mexico Press, 2001, 263–76.

Al-Hoda, 1898–1968: The Story of Lebanon and Its Emigrants as Taken from the Newspaper Al-Hoda. New York: Al Hoda Press, 1968.

Allen, Paula Francis and E. Lee Francis. "Yo cruso siete mares." *Confluencia* 1, no. 2 (1976): 19.

Armenta, Steve. "Cerrillos: A Story of Survival. " *La Herencia* 18, Summer 1998, 22–23.

Aryain, Ed. *From Syria to Seminole: Memoir of a High Plains Merchant*. Lubbock: Texas Tech University Press, 2006.

Barrington, Jackie, ed. *Magdalena: Celebrating One Hundred Years of Frontier Living.* Magdalena, New Mexico: Magdalena Old Timers' Association, 1984.

Bernstein, Joel H. "Magdalena's Salome Store: A Living Link to Cowtown Days." *New Mexico Magazine* 77, no. 4 (April 1999): 66–67.

Ellis, Raff. *Kisses from a Distance: An Immigrant Family Experience.* Seattle: Cune Press, 2007.

History of Torrance County. Estancia, New Mexico: Torrance County Historical Society, 1979.

Hughes, Debra. "Mom & Pop Stores Offer Slice of Hospitality." *New Mexico Magazine* 75, no. 5 (November 1997): 36–41.

"Into the Fabric of Santa Fe: The Salmons and the Greers." *The Santa Fean Magazine* 6, no. 4 (1978): 15–18.

Maaloof, Amin. *Origins: A Memoir*, trans. By Catherine Temerson. New York: Farrar, Straus and Giroux, 2004.

Pacheco, Ana. "Abdallah Samuel Adelo." *La Herencia* 41, Spring 2004, 20–21.

Peña, Abe. *Memories of Cíbola.* Albuquerque: University of New Mexico Press, 1997.

Rihbany, Abraham Mitri. *A Far Journey.* Boston: Houghton Mifflin, 1914.

Sahd, Patricia L. and Theodore M. Sahd, eds. *The Sahd Family Recipes: An American Feast Lebanese Style*, 1986.

Southwest History Class. *Viva El Pasado: A History of the Bernalillo Area.* Bernalillo, New Mexico: Bernalillo High School, n.p., 1974–75.

Suleiman, Michael. "The Mokarzels' Contribution to the Arab-Speaking Community in the United States." *Arab Studies Quarterly* (March 22, 1999): 8–12 and passim.

Sullivan, Anne. "Magdalena's Salome Store—Doorway to the Past." *Southern New Mexico Travel and Tourism Information*, January 11, 2003.

Toothman, Susan. "From Zahle to Springer." *The Trader*, (July 25, 1979): 2, 7–8.

Twain, Mark. *The Innocents Abroad.* Modern Library Paperback Edition, 2003.

Valencia County Historical Society. *Rio Abajo Heritage: A History of Valencia County.* Belen, New Mexico: The Society, 1983.

Vigil, Arnold. "New Mexico's Lebanese Influence." *La Herencia* 39, Fall 2003, 16–18.

Wylder, Meldrum K. *Rio Grande Medicine Man.* Santa Fe: Rydal Press, 1958.

Secondary Works:

Alfaro-Velcamp, Theresa. *So Far from Allah, so Close to Mexico: Middle Eastern Immigrants in Modern Mexico.* Austin: University of Texas Press, 2007.

Akarli, Engin Deniz. "Ottoman Attitudes Towards Lebanese Emigration, 1885–1910. In Hourani, *The Lebanese in the World*, 109–138.

Allen, Paula Gunn. "Life Is a Fatal Disease," and "High Steppin' Seboyetano." *Life Is a Fatal Disease: Collected Poems, 1962–1995.* Albuquerque: West End Press, 1997.

———. "Paternity." *Shadow Country.* Los Angeles: UCLA Publication Services Department, 1982.

Ashabranner, Brent. *An Ancient Heritage: The Arab-American Minority.* New York: HarperCollins, 1991.

Becker, Carl L. "Everyman His Own Historian." *American Historical Review* 37, no. 2 (January 1932): 221–36.

Barkan, Robert Elliott. "Turning Turner on His Head? The Significance of Immigration in Twentieth-Century American Western History." *New Mexico Historical Review* 77, no. 1 (Winter 2002): 57–88.

Bodnar, John. "The Construction of Ethnic Memory." Chap. 3 in *Remaking America: Public Memory, Commemoration, and Patriotism in the Twentieth Century*. Princeton, NJ: Princeton University Press, 1993.

Boosahda, Elizabeth. *Arab-American Faces and Voices: The Origins of an Immigrant Community*. Austin: University of Texas Press, 2003.

Bourke, John G. "Notes on the Language and Folk Usage of the Rio Grande Valley (With Special Regard to Survivals of Arabic Customs)." *Journal of American Folklore* 9, no. 33 (1896): 81–116.

Christgau, Alice E. *The Laugh Peddler*. New York: Young Scott Books, 1968.

Chávez, Fray Angélico, *My Penitente Land: Reflections on Spanish New Mexico*. New Edition. Santa Fe: Sunstone Press, 2012.

Chávez, Tibo. *New Mexico Folklore of the Rio Abajo*. Portales, New Mexico: Bishop Printing, 1972.

Ciotola, Nicholas P. "From Agriculturalists to Entrepreneurs: Economic Success and Mobility Among Albuquerque's Italian Immigrants, 1900–1930." *New Mexico Historical Review* 74, no. 1 (January 1999): 3–27.

Clark, Anna Nolan. "Mothers of Cebolleta." *New Mexico Magazine* 15, no. 2 (February 1937): 17–19, 39–40.

Conklin, Nancy Faires and Nora Faires. "'Colored' and Catholic: The Lebanese in Birmingham, Alabama." In Hooglund, *Crossing the Waters*, 69–85.

Córdova, Lorenzo de. *Echoes of the Flute*. Santa Fe: Ancient City Press, 1972.

Crane, Leo. *Desert Drums: The Pueblo Indians of New Mexico, 1540–1928*. Glorieta, New Mexico: Rio Grande Press, 1972. First published in Boston: Little, Brown & Co., 1928.

Cuentos: Tales from the Hispanic Southwest. Selected and adapted in Spanish by José Griego y Maestas; retold in English by Rudolfo A. Anaya. Santa Fe: Museum of New Mexico Press, 1980.

Daniels, Roger. *Coming to America: A History of Immigration and Ethnicity in American Life*. 2nd ed. New York: Harper Perennial, 2002.

Davis, Ellis Arthur, ed. *Historical Encyclopedia of New Mexico*, vols. 1&2. Albuquerque: Albuquerque Historical Association, 1945.

Delgado, Casimira. "Who Were These Gypsies?" *La Herencia* 18, Summer 1998, 27.

Deutsch, Sarah. *No Separate Refuge: Culture, Class, and Gender on an Anglo-Hispanic Frontier in the American Southwest, 1880–1940*. New York: Oxford University Press, 1987.

Fergusson, Harvey. *The Conquest of Don Pedro*. New York: William Morrow, 1954.

García, Nasario, ed. *Comadres: Hispanic Women of the Río Puerco Valley*. Albuquerque: University of New Mexico Press, 1997.

———. *The Naked Rainbow and Other Stories*. Albuquerque: University of New Mexico Press, 2009.

Greer, Richard R. "Origins of the Foreign Born Population of New Mexico during the Territorial Period." *New Mexico Historical Review* 17, no. 4 (October 1942): 281–87.

Harris, William W. *Faces of Lebanon: Sects, Wars, and Global Extensions*. Princeton, NJ: Marcus Wiener Publishers, 1997.

Halaby, Raouf. "Dr. Michael Shadid and the Debate over Identity in the *Syrian World*." In Hooglund, *Crossing the Waters*, 55–69.

Higham, John. "The Problems of Assimilation in the 19th Century." *Journal of American Ethnic History* 1(1981): 7–25.

Hitti, Philip K. *A Short History of Lebanon*. New York: St. Martin's Press, 1965.

– – –. *The Syrians in America*. New York: George H. Doran, 1924.

Hooglund, Eric J., ed. *Crossing the Waters: Arabic-Speaking Immigrants to the United States before 1940*. Washington, DC: Smithsonian Institution Press, 1987.

Houghton, Louise Seymour. "Syrians in the U.S." *Survey: A Journal of Constructive Philanthropy* 26 (July–September 1911): 481–95, 647–65, 787–803; *Survey* 27 (October–December 1911): 957–68.

Hourani, Albert and Nadim Shehadi, eds. *The Lebanese in the World: A Century of Emigration*. London: I. B. Tauris, 1993.

Hurt, Wesley R. *Manzano: A Study of Community Disorganization*. New York: AMS Press, 1989.

Issawi, Charles. "British Trade and the Rise of Beirut: 1820–1860." *International Journal of Middle East Studies* 8, no. 1 (1977): 91–101.

– – –. "The Historical Background of Lebanese Emigration, 1800–1914." In Hourani, *The Lebanese in the World*, 13–31.

Jaehn, Tomas. *Germans in the Southwest, 1850–1920*. Albuquerque: University of New Mexico Press, 2005.

John, Sarah E. "Arabic-Speaking Immigration to the El Paso Area, 1900–1935." In Hooglund, *Crossing the Waters*, 105–118.

Keller, Tim. "Arabian Wind." *Western Horsemen*, September 2011: 76–79.

Khalaf, Samir. "The Background and Causes of Lebanese-Syrian Immigration to the United States before World War I." In Hooglund, *Crossing the Waters*, 17–37.

– – –. *Persistence and Change in 19th Century Lebanon*. Beirut: American University of Beirut, 1979.

Khater, Akram Fouad. "'House' to 'Goddess of the House': Gender, Class, and Silk in 19th Century Mount Lebanon." *International Journal of Middle East Studies* 28, no. 3 (1996): 325–48.

– – –. *Inventing Home: Emigration, Gender, and Middle Class in Lebanon, 1870–1920*. Berkeley: University of California Press, 2001.

Kayal, Philip M. and Joseph M. Kayal. *The Syrian-Lebanese in America: A Study in Religion and Assimilation*. Boston: Twayne Publishers, 1975.

Kelly, Daniel. *The Buffalo Head: A Century of Mercantile Pioneering in the Southwest*. Santa Fe: Vergara Publishing Company, 1972.

Larson, Robert W. *New Mexico's Quest for Statehood, 1846–1912*. Albuquerque: University of New Mexico Press, 1968.

Laudan, Rachel. "The Mexican Kitchen's Islamic Connection." *Saudi Aramco World* 55, no. 3 (2004): 32–39.

Lowenthal, David. *The Heritage Crusade and the Spoils of History*. Cambridge: Cambridge University Press, 1998.

Luebke, Frederick. "Ethnic Minority Groups in the American West." In *Historians and the American West*, edited by Michael P. Malone. Lincoln: University of Nebraska Press, 1983, 387–413.

Marín-Guzmán, Roberto. "Los inmigrantes árabes en Mexico en los siglos XIX y XX: Un estudio de historia social." In *El mundo árabe y América Latina*. Raymundo Kabchi, ed. Mexico City: J.

Nacif Mina en colaboración con el Instituto Cultural Mexicano Libanés, 1995. 123–53.

Nabhan, Gary. *Arab/American: Landscape, Culture, and Cuisine in Two Great Deserts*. Tucson: University of Arizona Press, 2008.

Nabti, Patricia. "Emigration from a Lebanese Village: A Case Study of Bishmizzine." In Hourani, *The Lebanese in the World*. 41–63.

Naff, Alixa. *The Arab Americans*. Juvenile edition. Philadelphia: Chelsea House Publishers, 1999.

———. "Arabs." In *Harvard Encyclopedia of America Ethnic Groups*, edited by Stephan Thernstrom, 128–136. Cambridge, Mass.:Belknap Press of Harvard University Press, 1980.

———. *Becoming American: The Early Arab Immigrant Experience*. Carbondale: Southern Illinois University Press, 1985.

———"Lebanese Immigration into the United States: 1880 to the Present." In Hourani, *The Lebanese in the World*, 139–48.

Nieto-Phillips, John M. *The Language of Blood: The Making of Spanish-American Identity in New Mexico, 1880s–1930s*. Albuquerque: University of New Mexico Press, 2004.

Nugent, Walter. "The People of the West Since 1890." In *The Twentieth Century in The West*, edited by Gerald D. Nash and Richard W. Etulain. Albuquerque: University of New Mexico Press, 1989, 35–70.

Orfalea, Gregory. *Before the Flames: Quest for the History of Arab-Americans*. Austin: University of Texas Press, 1988.

———. "There's a Wire Brush in My Bones." In Hooglund, *Crossing the Waters*, 173–185.

Parish, William. "The German Jew and the Commercial Revolution in Territorial New Mexico, 1850–1900." *New Mexico Historical Review* 35, no. 2 (April 1960): 129–143.

———. *The Ilfeld Company: A Study of the Rise and Fall of Mercantile Capitalism in New Mexico*. Cambridge, Mass: Harvard University Press, 1961.

Peña, Abe. *Villages and Villagers*. Los Ranchos de Albuquerque: Rio Grande Books, 2007.

Pugach, Noel. "New Mexico's Merchant Jews: Another Perspective," *Legacy* (March 2009): 2–3, 7.

Pulcini, Theodore. "Trends in Research on Arab Americans." *Journal of American Ethnic History* 12, no. 4 (Summer 1993): 27–60.

Rosenbaum, Robert. J. *Mexicano Resistance in the Southwest*. Dallas: Southern Methodist University Press, 1998.

Sabatino, Marcello. "The Arabic Element in Spanish," *The Arab World* (January–February 1963), n.p.

Salibi, Najib, "Emigration from Syria," *Arab Studies Quarterly* 3 (1981): 5–24.

Salloum, Habeeb. "Arabic Contributions to the Spanish Language." Electronic resource.

Seligman, G.L. "The El Paso and Northeastern Railroad's Economic Impact on Central New Mexico." *New Mexico Historical Review* 61, no. 3 (July 1986): 217–231.

Sellers, Maxine. "Beyond the Stereotype: A New Look at the Immigrant Women, 1830–1924." *Journal of Ethnic Studies* 3 (1975): 59–70.

Shakir, Evelyn. *Bint Arab: Arab and Arab American Women in the United States*. Westport, CT: Praeger, 1997.

———. "Good Works, Good Times: The Syrian Ladies' Aid Society in Boston, 1917–1932." In Hooglund, *Crossing the Waters*, 133–47.

Simmons, Marc. *New Mexico: A History.* New York, 1977.

Smith, Toby. "Arrows from Strong Bows," *New Mexico Magazine* 60, no. 2 (February 1982): 20–27.

Stoes, K. D. "Peddlers in the Old Frontier." New Mexico Magazine 29, no. 2 (February 1951): 22–50.

Suleiman, Michael W. "Early Arab Americans: The Search for Identity." In Hooglund, *Crossing the Waters,* 37–54.

———. "The Mokarzels' Contribution to the Arab-speaking community in the United States." *Arab Studies Quarterly.* March 1999.

Sweet, Linda Vozar. "The Sky's the Limit for Jemez Pioneers." *New Mexico Magazine* 75, no. 5 (May 1997): 22–25.

"Syrians in the United States," *Literary Digest 61,* no. 5 (1919): 43.

Tannous, Afif I. "Emigration, a force of social change in an Arab village." *Rural Sociology 7* (March 1942): 62–74.

Tobias, Henry J. A *History of the Jews in New Mexico.* Albuquerque: University of New Mexico Press, 1990.

Torres, Eliseo "Cheo" with Timothy L. Sawyer Jr. *Curandero: A Life In Mexican Folk Healing.* Albuquerque: University of New Mexico Press, 2005.

Tórrez, Robert J. *Myth of the Hanging Tree: Stories of Crime and Punishment in Territorial New Mexico.* Albuquerque: University of New Mexico Press, 2008.

Traboulsi, Fawwaz. *A History of Modern Lebanon.* London: Pluto Press, 2007.

Truzzi, Oswaldo M.S. "The Right Place at the Right Time: Syrians and Lebanese in Brazil and the United States, a Comparative Approach." *Journal of American Ethnic History* 16, no. 2 (Winter 1997): 3–34.

Twitchell, Ralph Emerson. *The Leading Facts of New Mexico History,* vol. 4. Cedar Rapids, IA: Torch Press, 1917.

Weigle, Marta and Peter White. *The Lore of New Mexico.* Albuquerque: University of New Mexico Press, 1988.

Wiegner, Kathleen and Robert Borden. *Jemez Springs.* San Francisco, CA: Arcadia Publishing, 2009.

Younis, Adele L. *The Coming of the Arabic-Speaking People to the United States.* Edited by Philip M. Kayal. Staten Island, NY: Center for Migration Studies, 1995.

Unpublished Materials: Dissertations, Theses, and Papers:

Adelo, A. Samuel. "Influence of Arabic in the Spanish Language. " Typewritten paper, n.d.

Bezirgan, Najm A. and Rosemary Gillett Karam. "The Cultural Heritage and Preservation of Syrian– Lebanese Traditions in the American Southwest." Typewritten manuscript in archives of Institute of Texan Cultures, University of San Antonio, San Antonio, Texas, 1973.

Caldwell, Thomas. "The Syrian-Lebanese in Oklahoma." M.A. thesis, University of Oklahoma, 1984.

Ciotola, Nicolas. "The Italians of Albuquerque, 1880–1930: A Study of Immigrant Adjustment and Assimilation." M. A. thesis, University of New Mexico, 1997.

DeMark, Judith Boyce. "The Immigrant Experience in Albuquerque, 1880–1920." PhD Dissertation, University of New Mexico, 1984.

Heath, Jim F. "A Study of the Influence of the Atchison, Topeka, and Santa Fe Railroad Upon the Economy of New Mexico, 1878–1900." M.A. thesis, University of New Mexico, 1955.

Hurt, Wesley Robert. "Manzano: A Study of Community Disorganization." M.A. thesis, University of New Mexico, 1941.

John, Sarah Elizabeth. "'Trade Will Lead a Man Far': Syrian Immigration to the El Paso Area, 1900–1935." M.A. thesis, University of Texas at El Paso, 1982.

Palmer, Mo. Transcribed interview by Geraldine Snow. The Albuquerque Museum of Art and History, 1990s.

Name Index

Abdalla, Nicolas, 40, 45, 46, 70-71, 97, 124
Abousleman, Edna, 102, 105, 121, 151-52
Abousleman family, 54, 103, 105, 119
Abousleman, George, 27, 105, 124, 139
Abousleman, Joseph, 27
Abousleman, Margarita Maestas, 105
Abousleman, Moses, 40, 94, 101-05, 141
Abousleman, Ron, 139-41
Abousleman, Tom, 103, 104
Adelo, A. Samuel, 45, 106, 108, 113, 122
Adelo family, 54, 109
Adelo, Lourdes Varela Silva, 107
Adelo, Samuel (Assad Abdullah Abu Habib), 107-09, 123, 124
Alfaro-Velcamp, Theresa, 32, 48
Allen, Paula Gunn, 78-79
Amin, Fred (Fuad Ameen), 54, 72, 73, 109
Amin, John, 45, 73, 122
Amin, Labibe Merhige, 72, 73
Atencio, Jeanetter Salome, 69
Azar, Adele, 27, 52, 148
Azar family, 44, 45, 113
Azar, Habeb, 113
Azar, Helen Michael, 94

Batchen, Lou Sage, 49
Beale, Edward Fitzgerald, 51
Bellamah, Anise, 141-43
Bellamah, Dale (Abdullah), 141-43
Bellamah, Naguib, 40, 86, 124, 141
Blatty, William P., 43
Bonahoom, Charles, 113
Bourke, John G., 116-17
Budagher family, 54, 119
Budagher, Joseph (Joseph Mansour Abu Dagher), 11, 44, 89, 94-98, 104, 140

Budagher, Sallie Faris, 94, 95, 97, 152-53

Calles, Plutarco Elias, 52
Casaus, Teodoro, 41
Chávez, Dennis, 94
Chávez, Fra Angélico, 122
Chávez, Tibo, 123
Christgau, Alice E., 44
Clark, Anna Nolan, 76
Cory, Elias, 113
Coury, Anton, 66-67
Coury, Gabriel, 66
Coury, Rafnaa Elias, 66, 67, 150
Crane, Leo, 96

David, Sleman (Sleman David Nsayer), 111-12
Davis, Ellis Arthur, 130
Delgado, Casimira, 49
DeMark, Judith, 36
Dillon, Richard, 96

El Khoury, John D.S., 36
Elias, 51-52

Fandey, Zaid, 72, 74
Farah, Mansour, 143
Farah, George, 144
Faris, Seth (Said), 89, 94
Fergusson, Harvey, 48
Fidel, A.H. (Abdoo Habib Fadel), 83-86
Fidel, Clara Salome, 69-70
Fidel family (Fadel), 37, 74, 126
Fidel, John, 27, 134-38
Fidel, Joseph, (Grants), 84, 85
Fidel, Joseph, (Las Vegas), 109-10

Fidel, Joseph, (Santa Fe), 133-38, 149
Fidel, Latife Hanosh, 84
Fidel, LouDelle, 27, 136
Fidel, Rose Ashkar, 149
Fidel, Toufic, 135-38
Fram family, 113
Francis, E.Lee II, 54, 76, 77, 78, 80, 117, 125
Francis, E. Lee IV, 80
Francis, Elias (Elias Francis Abu Hassan),
    27, 36, 44, 45, 53-54, 75-80, 120, 123
Francis family, 74-80, 119
Francis, Filomena Michael, 80
Francis, Narciso, 75, 76, 77, 79-80, 124-26
Francis, Pauline Hanosh, 75, 78, 80
Freye, Tanous, 40
Friedman, Meyer, 41

Gabor, Zsa Zsa, 133
Gabriel, John, 36
García, David F., 99
García, Nasario, 45, 50, 76
Goldenberg, Hugo, 41
Goze, George, 71-72, 124
Grant, Ulysses S., 23
Greer, E. John, 131, 132

Hadji, Ali (Hi Jolly), 51
Hanosh, Elias, 81
Hanosh family, 74, 126
Hanosh, John, 81-82, 83, 109
Hanosh, Joseph, 77, 80-81, 82
Hanosh, Malulia Salamy, 81, 82
Hanosh, Rose Fidel, 82-83, 110
Harp, Assad and Wardie, 74
Hilton, Conrad, 132, 133
Hindi, Alex (Ali), 61, 63, 64, 65, 124
Hindi, Brahaim, Sr., 64
Hindi, Clarita Duran, 63, 64
Hindi family, 44, 45, 60-65, 126
Hindi, Kassem, 61
Hindi, Rasmieh, 27, 63, 121
Hindi, William (Milhelm), 47, 61, 63, 65
Hitti, Philip, 26
Horton, Louise Seymour, 44
Huber, Oscar, 150
Hurt, Wesley R., 58

Hyder, Latif Mama, 128-29, 139

Ilfeld, Charles, 41, 49, 107
Ilfeld, (Los Lunas), 45

Jaehn, Tomas, 11

Keleher, W.H., 132
Keloff family, 113
Khalaf, Samir, 117
Khater, Akram, 29
Kouri, Albert Abraham, 113
Kouri, Joseph, 113
Koury, Gabriel, 96, 97
Koury, George and Mary, 100
Koury, James, 40, 145
Koury, John Ashkar, 41
Koury, K., 72
Koury, Marie Salome Joseph, 41, 100-101,
    121
Koury, Michael David, 40, 41, 89, 100

Lamadrid, Enrique, 99
Lowenthal, David, 118

Macaron family, 111-12
Macaron, Fred, 111
Macaron, Lilly, 111
Mahboub, Frida, 96
Mahboub, Lazarro and Nellie, 100
Maloof family, 41, 44, 45, 113, 139
Maloof, George, 138
Maloof, Helima, 150
Maloof, Joe, 140
Maloof, Obaid, 138
Mama (Hyder), Salim, 128-29
Martinez, Reyes, 50
Mechem, Edwin, 79
Mendes, Salada, 41
Merhige, Fidel, 109, 110-111, 140
Merhige, Latify, 148-49
Merhige, Mike, 110
Michael, Azize, 89, 93-94, 140
Michael, Doña Meme (Tameme), 86, 87, 152
Michael family, 40, 74, 109, 126
Michael, Filomena, 80

Michael, Merhige, 86-88, 120, 123, 124, 141
Michael, Rasheed, 36, 80, 89, 93-94
Michael, Simon, 40
Michael, Toby, 87, 152

Nabhan, Gary, 122, 123
Naff, Alexis, 12, 43, 44, 45
Nassif, Joe (Agag M.), 129
Nordhaus, Max, 41

Owen (Aoun), Alex, 92-93

Parish, William, 48-49
Peña, Abe, 74, 78, 87, 126, 127, 152
Peña, Abelicio, 86

Roosevelt, Theodore, 23
Rouckus, Mack, 133-34

Sahd (Saad), Abdo Youssef, 52, 89
Sahd, Clara Merhige, 52, 90, 150-51
Sahd, Gabriel and Jay, 90, 150-51
Sahd family, 37, 40, 52-53, 89, 109
Sahd, Fitty, 90, 108, 150
Sahd, Peter A., 53, 90-92
Sahd, S. Peter, 92
Sahd, Ted, 56, 90
Salmon, Nathan,(Na'aman Soleiman Farah) 40, 44, 45, 101, 109, 129-33, 139
Salmon, Salome, 131
Salome, George, 68
Salome family, 68-70, 124
Salome, Fred, 69
Salome, Jill, 69
Salome, Joe, 68
Salome, Morgan, 69
Seligman, Arthur, 96, 136
Seller, Margaret, 149
Shakir, Evelyn, 147, 148
Shaya, Raymond, 66, 124, 127. 144-45
Shepherd, Josephine Abousleman, 103
Silva, Dolores Gallegos, 98-99
Silva, Felix (Ferris Shaheen [Hyder]), 89, 98
Silva, Felix, 99, 140
Silva, George, 99-100
Silva, James, 100, 139

Skaff family, 113
Smith, Toufic (Toufic Haddad), 113
Sotel, Lilian Abousleman, 103
Stapp, William H., 48-49
Stoes, K.D., 50

Tabet, Abraham, 56
Tabet, Anisa, 57
Tabet, Carlos, 56, 59-60
Tabet, Elias, 57
Tabet family 40, 56-60, 119, 140
Tabet, Farida, 57
Tabet, Juan (Akel), 57
Tabet, Khalil (Calixo), 57
Tabet, Nassif, 56
Tabet, Onesima García, 59
Tabet, Samuel K., Sr., 57
Tabet, Samuel K., Jr., 57
Tabet, Severa Gonzales, 57
Tabet, Tannous, 56, 58
Tingley, Clyde, 94, 97, 132
Tobias, Henry, 11
Torres, Eliseo "Cheo", 120
Twain, Mark, 23
Twitchell, Ralph Emerson, 129

Younis, Adele, 41
Younis family, 37
Younis (Unes), Regis and Rufina, 40, 106
Younis, Tobias and Gabriel, 40, 106, 124

Weigle, Marta, 48, 117
Wylder, Meldrum, 120

Ziede, Antonio, 100

www.ingramcontent.com/pod-product-compliance
Lightning Source LLC
Chambersburg PA
CBHW020052170426
43199CB00009B/259